FIXING **BROKEN**
MEETINGS

FIXING
BROKEN
MEETINGS

A Manual on Meeting Rotten-osity, Deleterious Decisions, and Ineffective Implementation

JOHN TROPMAN, DANIEL MADAJ, AND CAROLYN GIER
University of Michigan, Ann Arbor

cognella®
SAN DIEGO

✿ cognella® | ACADEMIC PUBLISHING
3970 Sorrento Valley Blvd., Ste. 500, San Diego, CA 92121

BRIEF CONTENTS

DETAILED CONTENTS

PART IV ## To Decide or Not to Decide, That Is the Question

Chapter 9 ## Decision Avoidance Psychosis   59

PART V ## Decision Debacles, Drift, Difficulties, Delays, and Disruptions

Chapter 10 ## Decision Rotten-ocity and Partialization   67

PART VIII   **Bringing Home the Bacon:
Evaluation, Implementation, Launch,
Institutionalization, and
Refurbishment   113**

Chapter 16   Implementation   119

Chapter 17   The Evaluation   133

WEB-BASED RESOURCES:
ACCESSING QR CODES AND LINKS

The authors have selected some supporting web-based content for further engagement with the learning material that appears in this text, which can be accessed through QR codes or web links. These codes are intended for use by those who have purchased print copies of the book. You may scan them using a QR code reading app on your cell phone, which will take you to each website. You can also search for the link using a web browser search engine. Readers who have purchased a digital copy of the book can simply click on the hyperlinks beneath each QR code.

Cognella maintains no responsibility for the content nor availability of third-party links. However, Cognella makes every effort to keep its texts current. Broken links may be reported to studentreviews@cognella.com. Please include the book's title, author, and 7-digit SKU reference number (found below the barcode on the back cover of the book) in the body of your message.

Please check with your professor to confirm whether your class will access this content independently or collectively.

cognella®
SAN DIEGO

PREFACE

John Tropman

This book is about meetings, decision-making, implementation, and evaluation. It is new in structure. As an "anthology," there is usually a collection of articles and essays bound together with an introduction and commentary, as appropriate.

In this book, we provide synopses of 67 articles and books (as well as internet links where available). The original book was clocking in at over 500 pages, and the cost of permissions to reprint was becoming prohibitive. This slimmer volume is more accessible and less costly. Along the same lines, we provide descriptions (and link information) to 17 representative cartoons at the beginning of each chapter.

John E. Tropman wrote most of the introductory material, and Carolyn Gier and Dan Madaj, most of the synopses.

The volume began as a collection of humorous articles on meetings, but, as projects do, its focus expanded as ongoing research provided fresh information from those who were consistently excellent at those efforts. Much of the impetus for this book rose from the Meeting Masters Research Project, originally funded by the 3M Company and the University of Michigan School of Social Work. Over time, it evolved into the Decision Maestros Research Project and now has emerged as the High-Quality Policy Research Project with a focus on meetings, decisions, and socially-just policy.

That is on the practical side.

On the theoretical side, the excellent organizational practices team also gave some thought to "explaining" WHY meetings were so bad so often, why decisions were deeply flawed, why implementation fumbled, and why evaluation is rare.

Our core hypothesis is that meetings have at least four latent functions, as Robert Merton would call them (Merton 1968).

One function—fake meetings—is to fill the temporal office interstices within the workday/week/month when work can't be done with apparent work. (This phenomenon is detailed in the chapter on "bullshit jobs," Chapter 13).

The second function is that "meetings" are used by incompetent managers to display their power, humiliate enemies, appear competent, and generally express what we call power-peacocking.

The third function is that managers deliberately construct meaningless meetings so that, given the discussion and disagreement that result, they can say, "Well, since we all cannot agree, here is what we will do!"

The fourth is a result of managerial laziness or incompetence.

Reference

Merton, Robert. 1968. *Social Theory and Social Process.* Glencoe: Free Press.

INTRODUCTION

John Tropman

S uccess in life involves identifying the issues and concerns lying on "the road we are on or ahead" (or both), developing ideas about how to define them, making decisions about how to address them (the decision mosaic), implementing those decisions successfully as they morph into programs, and evaluating those decisions concerning their successes or failures and any surprising benefits or costs which might have occurred.

Thinkers have identified the phases of this process. In the 1950s, Harvard sociologist Talcott Parsons developed the **AGIL Table**— Adaptation, Goal Attainment, Integration, and Latent Pattern Management. "Adaptation" is defined as the "response to or manipulation of the external environment." "Goal attainment" is defined as the "definition and achievement of primary function(s)." "Integration" is defined as "oversight and coordination of parts or functions." "Latent pattern management" is defined as "cultural patterns that sustain and refresh motivation for action."

W. Edwards Deming developed a similar four-fold process called the **Plan-Do-Check-Act Cycle**, whereby planning (identifying your problems) leads to doing (testing potential solutions), which leads to checking (studying results), which leads to acting (implementing the best solution). The cycle then continues.

Garvin and Tropman have offered a **three-step model of the action sequence** in helping individuals, groups, families, communities, organizations, polities, societies, and the global/world change. It has three phases: beginning, middle, and end. Upon reflection, it appears that the four-phase model is more appropriate, and, indeed, viewed from a practical perspective, the "middle phase" is two phases and fits into the decision and implementation parts of the previous models. Hence, the fuller model would be the Beginning Phase (problem exploration) > Decision Phase (developing a strategy of decisions) > Action Phase (executing / implementing) > Ending Phase (episode termination).

Another model, called the **Competing Values Model**, was developed by Robert Quinn and Jeff DeGraff from the University of Michigan. It can be applied to individuals, organizations, and behaviors, and it can also serve as an organizational strategy. It is outlined below. The model is also divided into four quadrants; clockwise from the top left, they are to: Collaborate (do things together), Create (do things first), Compete (do things fast), and Control (do things right). People are at the very center of the circle, with an outer rung named "practice" and the outmost rung named "purpose." The word "flexible" is above the circle, at the top, with "external" at the right, "focused" at the bottom, and "internal" at the left. In between these four terms, along the outer edge of the circle, are the words "long-term development" (upper left), "breakthrough" (upper right), "short-term performance" (bottom right), and "incremental" (bottom left).

Another version of this model features styles of behavior, which characterize organizational "types," arranged in four boxes, two by two. The upper left box is labeled "Clan Oriented" (a very personal place like an extended family, mentoring, nurturing, participation); the upper right box is labeled "Adhocracy Oriented" (dynamic and entrepreneurial, people taking risks, values innovation, and entrepreneurship); the lower left box is labeled "Market Oriented" (results-oriented, getting the job done, values competition, and achievement); and the lower right box is labeled "Hierarchically Oriented" (favoring structure and control, coordination and efficiency, and in which stability is important). Four terms are listed at the top and bottom and to the left and right, with arrows pointing to them: "Flexibility and Discretion" at the top, "External Focus and Differentiation" at the right, "Stability and Control" at the bottom, and "Integral Focus and Integration" at the left.

Other applications of this model feature types of organizational culture and focus. The creating organization is the adhocracy in which the collaborating organization is the clan, the control organization is the bureaucracy, and the competing organization is the market organization.

Their organizational presentation always uses this positionality. How-ever, if we approach it from an action perspective and flip "control" and "compete," we would have Create > Collaborate > Compete > Control.

We have also developed a four-fold process, beginning with "problem-defining meetings" (referencing the Meeting Masters) and proceeding to decision-building (referencing the Decision Maestros), implementation (referencing the "implementation quarterback," quartermaster, and task force), and evaluation (referencing overseers and an auditor).

While our colleagues use a box design, we prefer a circle design that better communicates motion and exists over time. So, a circle called "problem-defining meetings" slightly overlaps a circle called "decision-building meetings," which slightly overlaps a circle called "implementation meetings," which slightly overlaps a circle called "eval-uation meetings." We also suggest a feed-forward process. None of us indicated that the team composition may change (and most always does) as the process migrates from one circle into another. Circles intersect to indicate that there is overlap or a "transition process" as the issue moves from one process to the next. Sometimes, this is even in the same meeting or, at other times, a preliminary recommendation decision (or option) is made in the initial meeting and forwarded to another group for a decision.

The material (both literature and research findings) in this work was developed through the Meeting Masters Research Project and the Decision Maestros Research Project at the University of Michigan. It was partially funded by the Meeting Management Institute at the 3M Company.

Much time was spent over the past 30 years looking at individuals who led very successful efforts in group activity from meetings (Meeting Masters) to taking the discussion to a conclusion (Decision Maestros) to implementing the decision in the appropriate venues by turning the decision (or policy) into programs (Implementation Quartermasters/Quarterbacks) to those who assessed the results/impact of the program.

This volume focuses mostly on their meetings and their discontents. A bad start almost always presages problems down the road.

The collection is called a meeting syllabus because, like a modern course syllabus, it contains the titles of articles of interest along with some original text. The articles are not themselves present as they would be in a typical anthology. Rather, links to them are provided (electronic, when possible, or otherwise, bibliographic). Some chapters are introduced with the description of a cartoon, which is similarly insourced.

This collection is divided into eight parts and 17 chapters.

1. **Part 1** deals with "meetings" and their various discontents. It contains some humorous pieces that illustrate the pattern of making fun of meetings and disparaging their utility.
2. **Part 2** addresses decision accomplishment/non-accomplishment.
3. **Part 3** provides some coping strategies.
4. **Part 4** provides some helpful tips for producing efficient meetings and building effective decisions.
5. **Part 5** addresses "decision avoidance psychosis" and considers why the support for remedial actions increases as proximity to the decision point increases.
6. **Part 6** provides some explanations of why we at all levels of the social organization accept such a flawed system. Sociologically, if a practice exists full of manifest dysfunctions, there must be significant latent functions it is serving. This section also includes a cautionary tale focusing on the idea of not underestimating people's commitment to rotten practices (a commitment strengthened by latent functions).
7. **Part 7** offers some potentially useful practices from the Meeting Masters and Decision Maestros.
8. **Part 8** considers some of the issues in implementation and evaluation.

References

Cameron, Kim S., Robert E. Quinn, Jeff DeGraff, and Anjan V. Thakor. 2006. *Competing Values Leadership: Creating Value in Organizations.* Northampton, MA: Edward Elgar Publishing.

Deming, W. "The Deming Institute. Enriching society through the Deming philosophy." https://deming.org/explore/pdsa/.

Garvin, Charles, and John E. Tropman. 1992. *Social Work in Contemporary Society* (Second Edition). New York: Allyn and Bacon. (Politics and world/global action systems were not in the original volume. One example of an international organization dedicated to change was DAVOS, a large international meeting of elites. It was canceled in 2020.)

Parsons, Talcott. 1970. *The Social System*. London: Routledge and Kegan Paul Ltd.

Tropman, John E., and Kathryn A. Kozaitis. 1991. *Playing by the Rules: Meeting the Challenge of High Quality Decisions*. Austin: 3M Meeting Management.

ACKNOWLEDGMENTS

All books are the product of many hands. The acknowledgments are like the running credits at the end of a movie. And everyone is important, from the star to the grip. I owe a big deal of appreciation to my wife Penny, whose occasional question, "How is the book coming?" provided constant stimulus. Dan has been involved in many of my projects over many years. Carolyn started on the project early on, moved on, and then rejoined when her schedule permitted. It is a great team, and each of you has been a fantastic collaborator.

Special thanks is owed to Cognella Academic Publishing, and our editor, Kassie Graves. Additionally, I want to thank professional colleagues such as James Blackburn, at the University of Michigan School of Social Work, Richard Edwards, Chancellor Emeritus of Rutgers and Dean of the School of Public Health at Louisiana State University Health Sciences Center, and Terry Mizrahi, Professor at Silberman School of Social Work and co-editor of *The Encyclopedia of Macro Social Work*. — *John Tropman*

Shortly after starting work in the U-M School of Social Work Dean's Office in 1974, I transcribed a letter for John Tropman, then noted that an innocent turn of phrase might be misinterpreted. We both laughed and laughed. It's been my distinct pleasure to still be working and laughing with John today! It's also been a pleasure working with Carolyn on this book; I worked at the School for 11 years but did not overlap with her student days. I'd also like to thank my son Nat and my daughter Emily, two humorous and wonderful outcomes of past married life! — *Daniel Madaj*

My deepest gratitude to John and Dan for reconnecting with me on this project; life is full of wonderful surprises! I admire your talent and work ethic, it has been an immense honor for me to work with you on this book. A special thank you to my husband, Mark, for his continued love and support and to my family, especially Tiffany, Katie, Laura, Stephanie, Ryan, and friends that make life so much fun. — *Carolyn Gier*

PART I

Meetings

*Where We Take Minutes
to Waste Hours*

"We only have a few rules around here,
but we really enforce them."

M eetings enjoy a nearly universal lack of popularity. In the now-dated training film *Meetings, Bloody Meetings* (all men, most smoking), actor John Cleese is involved with a participant in a failed and hysterically funny conversation. The member says to Cleese something like "Well, it's always good to get together," to which Cleese mutters *sotto voce*, "To see if there is any point in having gotten together."

In meetings in Japan, the hierarchical deference norms often prohibit those of lesser status to engage in truth-telling to those above them. The Japanese have developed two fixes for this problem. One involves after-work drinking among colleagues, during which important information can be passed along under the guise of inebriation. The second one is the Ringi System, in which very junior people make the rounds of meeting participants and get relevant information, which is then collated and presented to the larger group with no names attached (Srilalitha, 2015).

Reference

Sagi, Srilalitha. 2015. "Ringi System: The Decision Making Process in Japanese Management Systems: An Overview." *International Journal of Management and Humanities (IJMH)*, Volume 1, Issue 7, April.

CHAPTER 1

Meeting Rotten-ocity

Introduction

Meetings, meetings, meetings. "I got no work done today; I spent it all in meetings" is a frequent refrain.

This specific issue was outlined on May 15, 2022, in a "Social Q's" (social questions) column by Phillip Galanes in the *New York Times*. A questioner wrote in with the following lament:

> I work in a nonprofit that provides health care to low-income individuals and families. ... I love my job and my colleagues. The problem? We are inundated with nonstop employee meetings from 9–5 PM every day.

Galanes titles the query "No Time for Real Work."

While Covid may have changed our relentless meeting behavior, Zoom is rapidly filling in. One school system in Michigan went back to "coming into the office" only to have employees Zoom with others who were also in the office.

Meetings have a bad rep. John Tropman's uncle used to call his wife "The Committee." As a kid, John could not understand the insult—but it contains the constraint that committees place upon us and the lack of utility as well. Meeting jokes are the "gallows humor" of the corporate/organizational world. This opening section presents three of many humorous essays that focus on different elements of meeting madness.

The art world has not been free of its contribution either. The *New Yorker* Cartoon Bank has dozens of cartoons, many representing the dysfunction/malfunction of meetings and committees. We open each chapter with a representative cartoon.

Meetings cost a lot. The time spent in meetings and then meeting again is astronomical. If one wishes, there is a "meeting clock" available that tallies up the cost of a meeting (see the "meeting cost calculator and clock" at techcrunch.com).

In this chapter, we share brief synopses of two examples or examinations of "rotten" meetings. Dave Barry humorously describes "two major kinds of meetings" and gives "advice" on how to survive them. John Bonini lists five things that can go wrong in a "reporting" meeting and then suggests an alternative.

The Essential Idea:
How to Attend a Meeting

from *Claw Your Way to the Top: How to Become the Head of a Major Corporation in Roughly a Week*
by Dave Barry

Barry suggests that the modern business meeting might be better compared with a funeral, "in the sense that you have a gathering of people who are wearing uncomfortable clothing and would rather be somewhere else."

He says there are two major kinds of meetings: first, meetings held because it's a tradition to hold them. Barry says that "this type of meeting operates the way *Show and Tell* does in nursery school, with everybody getting to say something." Barry says the difference is that in nursery schools, "the kids actually have something new to say." Barry suggests, at your turn, to say that "you're still working on whatever it is you're supposed to be working on." Barry notes that the meeting would be over in five minutes if the chair simply asked, "Everybody who is still working on what he or she is supposed to be working on, raise your hand!" A second kind of meeting has "some alleged purpose." Sometimes the purpose is harmless, like "somebody wants to show slides of pie charts and give everybody a copy of a big fat report," but sometimes your "input" is requested. Barry says this request is made to "make sure that in case whatever it is turns out to be stupid or fatal, you'll get some of the blame."

Barry also gives humorous advice on how to "take notes," suggesting the drawing of doodles and interlocking rectangles.

The Essential Idea:
5 Reasons Why Reporting Meetings Are Awful (& What to Do Instead)
by John Bonini

WEB LINK: https://tinyurl.com/2s4y5wcc

Bonini defines a reporting meeting as a meeting to report on "aggregate data otherwise hard to measure in real time." He offers five reasons why these meetings are "awful," by which he means that they're stale, reactive, and unproductive.

1. **It's too late to act.** Performance can be improved by instilling a "culture of continuous learning and improvement" rather than waiting for a meeting at the end of the month to find out a goal has been missed.
2. **Data is not accessible to everyone** but usually only to executives and/or the members of the leadership team. "Consequently, the vast majority of people doing the work ... aren't sure how to improve the work they're doing."
3. **Data is vulnerable to spin.** Bonini says spin can happen when the ones with a voice in a reporting meeting are responsible for the data, "not necessarily the work."
4. **Data is prone to error.** To make the data more trustworthy, make it accessible to everyone so that everyone can provide "valuable context as to why things are happening."

5. **Analysis is not taught.** When reports are shared at the end of the month rather than looking at "these things as they happen," there's less chance to make productive adjustments.

Bonini suggests an "Align, Analyze, Adjust" framework in which data is made accessible to everyone; people are aligned to the right goals and KPIs "to track progress toward them"; where performance data is available to everyone, providing an opportunity for "analysis, context, and correlation"; and where adjustments can be made when they matter most: "right now."

References

Barry, Dave. 1986. "How to Attend a Meeting." In *Claw Your Way to the Top: How to Become the Head of a Major Corporation in Roughly a Week*. Emmaus, PA: Rodale Press, p. 24–28.

Bonini, John. 2019. "5 Reasons Why Reporting Meetings are Awful (& What to Do Instead)." *Databox.com*, March 21. https://databox.com/why-reporting-meetings-are-awful.

Galanes, Philip, 2022. "No Time for Real Work," *New York Times*, May 15, Social Q's.

CHAPTER 2

God Is Watching You
A Historical Perspective

Introduction

Putting meeting issues in a historical, yet familiar context is one way to take the "sting" out of criticism and discomfort while still making the point. Our cartoon at the beginning of part I, points to the historical context of meeting disputations in a faculty. The selections use historical context to make a point about the lack of accomplishment in meetings but also serve to "shroud" meeting criticism in a cultural past that takes some of the "sting" out of the negativity that participants no doubt feel.

Articles in this chapter look at a Biblical committee analyzing a "draft statement on war and peace," at an argument against a committee-approach to Bible writing, at ways to create a meeting "free-for-all," and a more contemporary look at church meetings.

The Essential Idea:
How to Make Pruning Hooks Out of Spears
by Herman F. Reissig

Reissig imagines a conversation at a meeting of the "Hebrew Committee on Relations with Other Nations" in the year 800 AD. The group discusses a "draft statement on war and peace" from Isaiah, which we know from Isaiah 2:4 as "God shall judge between the nations, and shall decide for many peoples; and they shall beat their swords into ploughshares, and spears into pruning hooks; nation shall not lift up sword against nation; neither shall they learn war anymore."

The committee quibbles over the statement, suggests various changes, and then tables the "statement" until the next meeting.

One committee member complains that the statement is too long. Another suggests that "slingshots" be added to the list that includes pruning hooks and swords. Another finds the directive that "nation shall not life up sword against nation" to be "too positive," and suggests adding "in our opinion." Another thinks that a definition of who "we" are is needed, plus more information about Hebrew motives and objectives. Then there is a discussion about whether "we" can speak for "all Hebrews" and someone worries that if all spears were turned into pruning hooks there would be too many pruning hooks.

The Essential Idea:
Bible by Committee
by Willard Espy

Willard Espy humorously suggests that "the creative process … is meant to be a solitary exercise," and points out that God didn't hire a crew but "spent six days from morning to evening" creating heaven and earth.

The King James Version of the Bible, on the other hand, while the "champion of all literary works," was created by a committee "to prepare a more accurate yet more majestic translation." Espy says that 54 scholars worked on the translation, which he says makes it more like "a committee within a committee within a committee within a committee."

The Essential Idea: Raffi's Rules for
Non-Parliamentary Procedure
by Richard Hirsch

This essay depicts a 10-rule Jewish version authored by a rabbi for a humorous, very UN-parliamentary way to conduct a meeting of the minds. There is no need for a majority to make decisions or to ensure fairness in any way. Meetings become a free-for-all with little respect paid to participants.

A couple of my favorite Raffi's Rules include:

> 1) "POINT OF PERSONAL OUTRAGE—At any time during a meeting when a participant becomes extremely upset, he or she shall have the right to interrupt any other speaker, will not be required to wait for recognition from the chair, and has the obligation to speak at a volume considerably higher than required for normal conversation."

> 10) "POINT OF GRUDGE—Entitles the participant to raise an issue debated and decided by the group not less than 5 years earlier, for which the participant has not yet forgiven those involved. Example: I just want to remind this board that I was opposed to the idea of hiring a rabbi at all when it first came up 10 years ago."

Take a look, are Hirsch's ideas for conducting a meeting being used in today's current meeting climate?

The Essential Idea:
Your Board Is Not Your Enemy
by Natalie Hart

WEB LINK: https://bit.ly/3OX9WHN

In this piece, Hart is referring to church boards. The Rev. Julian Guzman proclaims, "Your Board is not your enemy. Take the time to build deep relationships with your Board." Ok, well why does it feel like they are your enemy, and HOW do you build a good working relationship?

Author of *The Five Dysfunctions of a Team*, Patrick Lencioni says, "Sometimes we view our success as a team by its lack of conflict, but … being able to work through conflict means that the team trusts each other, is willing to be accountable to each other, and wants to bring about good results—all things we want in our teams."

Lencioni's pyramid depicts the five dysfunctions, base to top.

1. **Absence of trust**—Without trust, there can be no conflict.
2. **Fear of Conflict**—Without conflict, there can be no commitment.
3. **Lack of Commitment**—Without commitment, there can be no accountability.
4. **Avoidance of Accountability**—Without accountability, there are no results.
5. **Inattention to Results**

The pyramid for a dysfunctional Christian organization might include an additional layer to the base, "**The Absence of Forgiveness. Without forgiveness, there can be neither trust nor freedom to fail.**"

"The crisis of leadership, I believe, is a crisis of forgiveness. Leaders are expected to lead without mistakes." Maybe that should be true of a GM or other large corporations as these leaders are being paid millions to know what they are doing and how to lead.

A church is a very different organization. Most people serve on these boards with no compensation, team training, or leadership skills. They are just trying to serve their respective churches. You are dealing with many different personalities, age differences, and backgrounds. Trust in each other is essential. There should be room to fail, forgive, forget, and move on! Remember, all board members share a commitment to the vision and mission of the church. Everyone, including the pastor, wants the church to thrive and grow. Conflict needs to be worked through with members who will stick around to do this. Everyone needs to share in this huge commitment to feel the presence of God here on earth. The gift of the Holy Spirit can help us when the going gets rough. We are assured that God forgives us when we make mistakes. We need to forgive ourselves, forgive our fellow board members, and trust in God.

References

Bridges, Kyin, K. 2021. "Can we learn management teaching from the Japanese Ringi process?" http//kyinbridges.com.

Cleese, John, and Antony Jay. 1976. *Meetings Bloody Meetings*. London: Video Arts.

Espy, Willard. 1977. "Bible by Committee," *Harvard Magazine*, May–June.

Hart, Natalie, "Your Board Is Not Your Enemy," Urban Church Leadership Center, gatheringsofhope.org, p. 1–12.

Hirsch, Richard. 2001."Raffi's Rules for Non-Parliamentary Procedure Specifically for the Orderly Conduct of Jewish Meetings." *Sh'ma*, March

Reissig, Herman F. 1963. "How to Make Pruning Hooks Out of Spears," *Harper's Magazine*, January.

CHAPTER 3

The Omnibus Report

Introduction

For a variety of reasons, meetings, which are supposed to create accomplishment, often block it or are used to block it. The status quo is a powerful, often unacknowledged, force in all our lives.

Hostility toward change is driven by "implicit bias" in the here and now. Matt Richt, in his *New York Times* piece, "We Have a Creativity Problem" (April 16, 2022), opines the following:

> But the emerging science of implicit bias has revealed that what people say about creativity isn't necessarily how they feel about it. Research has found that we actually harbor an aversion to creators and creativity; subconsciously, we see creativity as noxious and disruptive, and as a recent study demonstrated (Katz et al. 2022) this bias can potentially discourage us from undertaking an innovative project or hiring a creative employee.

"People actually have strong associations between the concept of creativity and other negative associations like vomit and poison," said Jack Goncalo, a business professor at the University of Illinois at Urbana-Champaign and the lead author of the new study. "Agony was another one."

The phrase "If it ain't broke, don't fix it" is a common one used to stop forward motion. The phrase could be, of course, "If it ain't broke, make it better," but who has ever heard that nostrum?

Four articles in this chapter consider what it means to say a "whole lot of nothing" in meetings; they humorously discuss the value of phantom "special committees," present an imaginary report to the American Medical Association about the "crisis" of medical care, and jocularly consider the use of vague language (so people can read into your statement what they want to hear).

The Essential Idea: The Panel Chairman's Report (Universal)
by Harold W. Williams

Harold Williams suggests that the meeting chairperson will respectfully recognize everyone and everything known to humankind but never does define the actual problem or address the solution that the meeting was called for. By the time the chairperson does get down to business and address the current problem or solutions, they state, "I see my time is up." Is this by design? Does the chairperson really not want to address the issues, or is the chairperson just that bad at time management and getting to the point?

In this piece, Williams does an excellent job of depicting how well someone can say a whole lot of nothing to the attendees in a meeting. It shows just how often valuable time is wasted in unproductive meetings, and decisions are never reached.

The Essential Idea: Report of the Special Committee
by Warren Weaver

Weaver humorously suggests a "simpler" way for an organization to determine whether it should expand a certain activity: sidestep the appointment of a "special committee" of experts and go right to a "summary report" made up of several generic, interchangeable elements.

These elements include stressing the importance of the activity, the need for its greater financial support, that new techniques are suddenly now available to advance the activity and that haste is needed to capture the new enthusiasm of relevant experts, and that "the Russians ... are far ahead of us."

The report will estimate a large "preliminary" sum of money for "initial capital facilities," but, of course, the sum will always prove to be too small and will need to be added to.

The Essential Idea:
A Report to the AMA
by Frank Getlein

In an imaginary report to the American Medical Association, Getlein complains about the "crisis" of medical care for "old folks," which he says will inevitably lead to universal health care. When "the frontiers of free enterprise" are fenced in by fee schedules and the like, Getlein claims, "the advance of medicine will grind to a halt."

Getlein claims that "big fees" have been necessary for the creation and development of "wonder drugs," antibiotics, and tranquilizers. This "new era of tranquility" began when Americans moved from country to town and no longer bartered with poultry and produce for their doctors' services but, instead, used cash. "Doctors moved from the lower-middle class to the middle-middle class to the upper-middle class. They got rich."

Getlein suggests "prefacing each consultation with little sermonettes on socialized medicine and the sanctity of the patient-doctor relationship." He says these sermonettes are extra-effective "when given while anesthesia is taking hold just before a major operation."

He also says it is vital, "of course," for doctors to keep up and increase payments to the AMA's Washington "lobby," which Getlein says is already the largest in town. Perhaps doctors can also add a surcharge to their patients' bills to help fight the "socializing threat."

The Essential Idea: Diagnosis and Evaluation for (Almost) All Occasions

by Alfred Kadushin

Alfred Kadushin suggests through three case studies that in psychological assessments the language is very vague. People can identify and are able to read their own meaning into the statements they receive and, therefore, the statement becomes "personal" to them. For instance, the most effective statements include the phrase "at times." Such as, "at times you feel anxious but other times you are confident about yourself." This phrase can apply to almost anyone and, therefore, each person can read a personal meaning into it.

Other hedging clauses include "generally," "on occasion," and "for the most part." As Kadushin indicates in these case summaries, there has become a "universal" diagnostic summary used for all. Only the names and a few details change. This is true of astrologers, palm readers, and pseudo-psychologists that people in need of counseling take their problems to. Kadushin warns not to be fooled by a psychic or a phony faith healer. Be skeptical. "Keep your money in your wallet, your wallet in your pocket, and your hand on your wallet." Oh, if we only could.

References

Getlein, Frank. 1963. "A Report to the AMA." In *A Stress Analysis of a Strapless Evening Gown, And Other Essays for a Scientific Age*, edited by Robert A. Baker, 117–121. Hoboken, NJ: Prentice-Hall, Inc.

Kadushin, Alfred. 1963. "Diagnosis and Evaluation for 'Almost' All Occasions." *Social Work,* Vol. 8, No. 1, January, 12–19.

Katz, Joshua H., Thomas C. Mann, Xi Shen, Jack Goncalo, and Melissa Ferguson. 2022. "Implicit Impressions of Creative People: Creativity Evaluation in a Stigmatized Domain." *Organizational Behavior and Human Decision Processes,* Vol. 169, March. (Science Direct: https://www.sciencedirect.com/science/article/pii/S0749597821001126).

Richt, Matt. 2022. "We Have a Creativity Problem." *New York Times*, April 16.

Williams, Harold W. 1959. "The Panel Chairman's Report (Universal)," *Harper's Magazine*, July.

Weaver, Warren. 1963. "Report of the Special Committee." In *A Stress Analysis of a Strapless Evening Gown, And Other Essays for a Scientific Age*, edited by Robert A. Baker, 150–155. Hoboken, NJ: Prentice-Hall, Inc.

CHAPTER 4

The Meeting Sciences
Applying Trivial Rigor

Introduction

There is not an empirically based "standard of care" for sick meetings. There is, however, a lot of written material, much of it anecdotal accounts of "I did it my way." A couple of these capture a high standard of conceptualization. One is "How to Run a Meeting" by Antony Jay and another is "The Medium of Managerial Work" by Andrew S. Grove (see our Chapter 14 for a synopsis of each).

The two pieces here apply trivial rigor to the task of committee evaluation, showing that too much of a good thing can be a bad thing and also funny.

One article humorously suggests that the ideal committee size is five people, and another humorously uses math to "study "the effectiveness of committees.

The Essential Idea: Directors, Councils, or (the) Coefficient of Inefficiency
from *Parkinson's Law and Other Studies in Administration*
by *C. Northcote Parkinson*

Parkinson believes committees fall into two categories: (1) those from which the individual member has something to gain and (2) those to which the individual member merely has something to contribute.

Committees or cabinets should ideally consist of five people. Throughout history, the growth of the English Cabinet went from five people in 1740 to 23 in 1939 and back to 18 in 1954. There are many disadvantages of trying to assemble a lot of people at the same date, time and place. The more members, the more it can make the whole meeting a waste of time. Whenever there are more than 20 members present, the meeting changes character and conversations develop separately at either end of the table. As Parkinson suggests, "the coefficient of inefficiency must lie between 19 and 22 is now very generally agreed." The interesting theory is that the best possible number of committee members must be eight members. Why you ask? That is the number all cabinets of countries of the world have avoided. Ok then, I will go with eight members, or better yet, Lucky 7.

The Essential Idea:
On (the) Mathematics of Committees, Boards, and Panels
by Bruce S. Old

Old uses various mathematical formulas to humorously "study" the efficiencies, or outputs, of committees, boards, and panels.

Old says it is "apparent" that in many cases membership should be "limited to one (person), and membership of over five is usually fatal." Old claims that research shows the peak efficiency of a committee's output is "seven-tenths of a person." He goes on to say that "either further research is required or … people are no damned good."

In "studying" the effect of the output of the intelligence of individual committee members, Old says the abilities of committee personnel can usually be reduced to two groups: knowledgeable, working-level personnel and ignorant, policy-level personnel. "Thus," Old says, "in forming a committee, one is confronted with the decision as to whether he wishes the membership to be composed of working- or policy-level personnel."

Old considers the capabilities of the committee chair. Some are capable, know the subject, are well-prepared, and keep people on-subject. Sometimes, capable chairs are "too nice," too hesitant to "interrupt ramblers, particularly if they happen to occupy a higher position or are older." Some use the committee "merely as an instrument to second their ideas." Some are "obviously too important for the committee," and send a deputy to "run" the meeting until the chair can "find times to attend and whip things into shape." Some don't know who called the meeting or what the purpose was of meeting today.

Old considers that sometimes committees with "intelligent members and a competent chairman" are ruined by "heckler-saboteurs," who include "the jolly fellow who is always 22 minutes late," "the man with an elephantine memory to whom all ideas are old," "the man who is against initiating any work" because of a shortage of manpower, "the poor fellow sent to represent his boss who has instructed him … (so) that all he can do is sit there," "the policy man who is afraid the rest of the committee is trying to take away some of his power and authority," and "the man who is on the defensive."

Old adds that sometimes "miscellaneous" factors can affect committee efficiency, such as when "a quorum of committee members happened to get together the night before … and settle all the expected controversies of the morrow in the bar."

References

Old, Bruce S. 1946. "On (the) Mathematics of Committees, Boards, and Panels." *Scientific Monthly* (now *Science*), Volume 63, August, 129–134.

Parkinson, C. Northcote. 1957. "Directors, Councils, or (the) Coefficient of Inefficiency." In *Parkinson's Law and Others Studies in Administration*, Chapter 2. Boston: Houghton Mifflin Co.

PART II

Impediments in Meetings

Behavioral, Power-Peacocking, and Institutional

"Helen, you're the Team Leader, why don't you jump first?"

There are numerous impediments to achieving accomplishment-based meetings and high-quality decisions. Blaming the participants is one. Power dynamics are a second. Racism and sexism are among a large range of discriminatory stereotypes featured here.

CHAPTER 5

Troublesome Types/ Troublesome Behavior

Introduction

One of the most common explanations for meeting problems involves the troubling personalities that are meeting participants and cause numerous problems both in the meeting and outside of it. This "blame the participants" strategy removes meeting planners from their lack of skill in agenda preparation, staging, and setting up the problems to be addressed. It also is a sort of shrug-of-the-shoulders approach that essentially says "Well, you know how Tim or Sheila is; there is nothing I can do about it." The cartoon at the beginning of Part II says it all; meeting participants are all cads. Each course has its peculiarities; some of us are more aware of them than others. However, if meeting "drama" has a well-organized "script" (the agenda) and associated materials which members have had time to read and think about in advance, the chances of meeting accomplishment are importantly increased.

One article humorously describes five "classic" roles in meetings, another article describes four types of academic "jerks," and a third article describes eight "committeeship" types. Another article promotes the idea of "pronoids," people (generally men) with delusions of grandeur and competence who have the opposite of paranoia. A final article describes the impact of a "troublesome type" in a real-world road commission meeting.

The Essential Idea: Meetings

from *The Dilbert Principle*

by Scott Adams

Adams suggests that "meetings are a type of performance art, with each actor taking on a role." He then describes five "classic" roles:

The **Master of the Obvious** "feels a responsibility to share his wisdom at every opportunity." A favored line of the Master: "We want a win-win solution." A "convincing Master" combines condescension with sincerity. Adams suggests practicing by repeatedly explaining to a lamp why electricity is essential and to keep practicing "until you can make a bulb burn out just by talking to it."

The **Well-Intentioned Sadist** "believes that meetings should hurt." Adams suggests several techniques for causing discomfort: excessively long meetings with no bathroom breaks and meetings at lunchtime or on Friday afternoon. Adams suggests getting in the right mood by showing "movies in which the star's family gets massacred and later his dog dies while taking a bullet for him."

The **Whining Martyr** gets "a lot of stage time." Adams suggests crafting "your complaints into tales that illustrate how valuable and intelligent you are compared to the obstructionist dolts who surround you." A suggested whine: "Boy, I'd love to be able to take sick days like you people who don't have work to do."

The **Rambling Man** redirects "any topic toward an unrelated event in which he participated." Adams says the point is primarily to "let everybody know how clever he is." Adams notes that rambling is different than babbling: "Unlike rambling, babbling is related to the topic, yet somehow it lasts a long time without conveying any useful information."

The **Sleeper** is "essentially a stage prop. There are no lines involved in this role." Adams suggests that if pressed to speak, to say things like "Same ol' same ol'" or "Uh huh."

The Essential Idea:
The Corporate Pronoids—A New Organizational Type?

by Fred Goldner

Pronoia is the logical opposite of paranoia, writes Fred Goldner, the

> "delusion that others think well of one. Actions and the products of one's efforts are thought to be well-received and praised by others who, when they talk behind one's back, must be saying good things, not bad. Mere acquaintances are seen as close friends. Politeness and the exchange of pleasantries are interpreted as expressions of deep attachment and the promise of future support."

Pronoia seems to be rooted in the social complexity and cultural ambiguity of our lives. We have become increasingly dependent on the opinions of others that are, in turn, based on uncertain criteria.

Goldner gives three examples of people with pronoia (all are men; Goldner suspects pronoia is "especially prevalent among men.") In one, a consultant is found to have consistently "distorted the reactions of others in a positive light" when writing reports of committee and other activity. In another, a high corporate official "referred to any influential person he had met once as a close personal friend" and also assumed "these people supported anything he had to say." They "seldom listened to others and assumed that others always agreed with him." In the third example, a university professor applying for tenure submitted a letter as "evidence of how well his own work was received." In fact, "the only positive aspects of the letter were the opening expression of interest and the closing sentence saying that Brown was involved in an interesting area of research and should keep the letter writer informed. The rest of the letter was a devastating critique of Brown's work."

Goldner suggests that pronoia can grow because "bosses generally avoid criticizing subordinates to their face, thus, leaving subordinates ignorant of negative evaluations," and expressions of anger by a boss may be brushed aside "precisely because they are displays of anger—that is, manifestations of a loss of control." Goldner notes that letters of recommendation are also a major cause of pronoia due to their "inflated language, their avoidance of negative factors, and their frequent equivocation."

The aggressive and argumentative character of some pronoids inhibits disagreement, Goldner says, partly because "one reacts to aggressive people the same way one usually reacts to a boor—with silence. One hesitates to respond for fear of encouraging the speaker to continue. Silence is the result, and silence is taken as agreement." Silence can also be seen as the absence of complaint. Goldner gives the example of an employee about to be fired who writes a memo about themselves, listing what they thought were their strengths; when the boss didn't comment about the memo, the employee thereby believed the boss agreed with it and was surprised when they did get fired.

The Essential Idea: The Jerks of Academe
by Eric Schwitzgebel[1]

WEB LINK: https://www.chronicle.com/article/the-jerks-of-academe/

Schwitzgebel gives a few hints about how to recognize four kinds of academic "jerks." They add that "jerks don't usually know that they are jerks. Jerks mostly travel in disguise, even from themselves."

The Big Shot can be spotted "a mile away. Their plumage is so grand! (Or so they think!) Their publications so widely cited! (At least by the right people)." "You will never full appreciate the Big Shot's genius, but if you cite him copiously and always defer to his judgment, he'll think you have above-average intelligence."

Eric Schwitzgebel, Excerpts from "The Jerks of Academe," *The Chronicle Review*, https://www.chronicle.com/article/the-jerks-of-academe/. Copyright © 2020 by The Chronicle of Higher Education. Reprinted with permission.

The Sadistic Bureaucrat is recognizable by "the little smile he can't quite suppress" as they apologize but "informs you that your reimbursement application was not completed correctly." They remind you that "the policies are clearly listed in the faculty manual." Even as they say it would be unfair to make an exception, "his friends don't seem to suffer under the policies in quite the same way."

The Creepy Hugger appears as the opposite of the Big Shot. "He will seem kind, modest, and charming, despite his impressive accomplishments. This is his alluring disguise." You will probably "encounter the type who takes advantage of his power to extract favors and 'friendship' that you would not otherwise give. ... Soon, he will be distracted by someone better and forget you exist—unless he can gain advantage by presenting you as his protégé."

The Embittered Downdragger is "unimpressed that you finally managed to publish in a so-called 'elite' venue. And your great teaching evaluations? They prove only that you cater to student demand for easy A's." The Embittered Downdragger "serves no important administrative role. This is because he knows that the system is corrupt. He rolls his eyes at the award you just won and the invitation you just received. His 'no' vote can be relied on for every policy change, every new initiative, and every tenure case."

Schwitzgebel says the central defining feature of jerkitude is "culpably failing to appreciate the perspectives of the people around you" and that the essence of being a jerk is "illegitimately devaluing others' goals and ignoring their opinions."

Schwitzgebel finds it so easy to imagine the inner life of these jerks because "it's my own inner life, sometimes. I catch myself thinking in these ways, and I worry. That sting of worry is the moral self-knowledge I treasure—the seeing that it is so, which makes it less so."

The Essential Idea: Committeeship

from *One-Upmanship*

by Stephen Potter

Potter defines "committeeship" as "the art of coming into a discussion without actually understanding a word of what anybody is talking about." He then describes eight committeeship types:

One type is highly positioned and perhaps a somewhat muddled chairperson, but never "in a flap" about their mistakes. Their excuses are "endearing" and Potter says the point of this type of member is "being adored by everybody."

A second type is "also rather mad," manic, with one shoe undone and a faint tremor in his left hand. "He is the permanently 'difficult' one," Potter says, and finds themselves in "definite disagreement" with the chair early on over some minor issue.

A third type is a "tremendously ordinary chap, valuable because he is in close touch with tremendously ordinary people and can, himself, talk tremendously ordinarily." Potter describes them as "the man in the street."

A fourth type is "totally new, of high value," developed "entirely through "Lifemanship-sponsored organi[z]ations." ("Lifemanship" is defined by *Merriam-Webster* as "the skill … of achieving … an appearance of superiority over others … by perplexing and demoralizing them.") Potter says they are "the man not in the street."

A fifth type is "not brilliant at all but sensible." Potter says they counter brilliant suggestions by saying, "Yes, but don't forget the big picture. What, after all, are we trying to sell?"

A sixth type "puts business first and says so. In the world of journalism, he is so hard-boiled about tender feelings that rival committeemen are thought to feel awe."

A seventh type can be "any of the foregoing, and yet none. He is the natural counter-committeeman, the underminer. It is not what he is, but what he says, that matters."

An eighth type differs from the others because "he knows, if possible, less about the subject under discussion, and the business of the committee generally, than anybody else present." Potter adds that this type "invariably creates an economics wicket by referring everything to the social or monetary sciences."

In several books, Robert Sutton describes "working with—and surviving—bullies, creeps, jerks, tyrants, tormentors, despots, backstabbers, egomaniacs, and all the other assholes who do their best to destroy you at work."

Sutton lists 12 "common everyday actions that assholes use," including personal insults, uninvited physical contact, and rude interruptions.

They list seven "techniques that are prone to fail and backfire," including using direct and aggressive confrontation, finding a scapegoat, or calling the asshole an asshole.

They list 12 "factors that encourage people to act like … assholes," including wielding power over others, especially if you once had little power, you are a "rule Nazi," or you are rich.

In addition, Sutton lists seven ways to be "part of the solution, not the problem," including using the daVinci rule (it's easier to resist at the beginning than at the end), protecting others (and not just yourself), and taking a look in the mirror, "Are you part of the problem?"

The Essential Idea: "Personal Attack" Mars Road Commission Meeting
by Eric Carlson

Carlson describes a meeting of the Leelanau County Road Commission, during which one of the commissioners opposed the purchase of a road grader, approved in the previous year's budget, but went on to say that their "disagreement" had to do with "someone not doing their job or capable of doing their job," and added that "there's government decisions being throwed [sic] out there with zero common sense."

This commissioner felt it best to wait to purchase the grader until next year when he thought the price would be lower. The commission's "fleet and facilities" officer countered by saying prices for similar items had gone up three percent last year, and said that it was "just impossible" to predict "what will happen to prices between now and next fall, but I don't expect them to decrease."

Another commissioner noted that "the process of soliciting competitive bids for the grader had taken months and were conducted in accordance with state laws guiding public agencies" and that stopping the acquisition process and then reopening it for later bids might give potential suppliers "an unfair advantage" and might result in legal challenges. This commissioner added that stopping the acquisition process and reopening it for bids would give other potential suppliers an unfair advantage and could result in legal challenges.

"That's as asinine a government deal as I've ever heard," the dissenting commissioner interjected. "Zero common sense!" Later in the meeting, they said, "I've calmed down a bit now. But I want the thinking around here to be more 'outside the box'" and less brown-nosing behavior.

References

Adams, Scott. 1997. "Meetings." *The Dilbert Principle*. New York: Harper Business.

Carlson, Eric. 2020. "'Personal Attack' Mars (Leelanau County, Michigan) Rd. Comm. Meeting." *Leelanau Enterprise*, Thursday, April 16, 10.

Goldner, Fred. 1982. "The Corporate Pronoid—A New Organizational Type?" *Social Problems*, Vol. 30, No. 1.

Potter, Stephen. 1977. "Committeeship." In *One-Upmanship*. London: Penguin Books. Chapter 3, pp. 41–57.

Schwitzgebel, Eric. 2020. "The Jerks of Academe." *The Chronicle Review*, February 14.

Sutton, Robert. 2010. *The No Asshole Rule: Building a Civilized Workplace and Surviving One That Isn't*. New York City: Grand Central Publishing.

_____. 2017. *The Asshole Survival Guide: How to Deal with People Who Treat You Like Dirt*. Boston: Houghton Mifflin Harcourt.

CHAPTER 6

The Perils of Power

Introduction

Meetings and committees are occasions for the acquisition and application of power. One way to think about power is that it is like a drug; it affects the brain itself. The more one has of it, the more one wants even more. Part of this "power addiction doom loop" comes from the fact that the application of power is likely to cause resistance, something that requires even more power to overcome. And so the cycle goes. The diminishment of the "great man" theory again hides the shields, in this case, the latent and manifest power dynamic.

One article humorously outlines ways to use meetings to cement your place in the hierarchy. Another considers the corruptive influence of power, and another shows us how mental "tricks" allow dictators to turn off compassion.

The Essential Idea: Meetings: Power-Sucking in a Group Atmosphere

from *The Below-the-Belt Manager*

by Eric Broder

Broder humorously outlines ways to use meetings for "further cementing the hierarchy (you up; everyone else down) in your organization." First, they suggest you set the agenda with this in mind: "This is my company and my meeting. Don't do or say anything that will make me hurt you." Second, they suggest staring at someone other than the person giving a report, which will make both people uncomfortable. Third, Broder likes to make others tense and uncomfortable with body language: "waving my hand in front of my face as if brushing away a fly, raising myself up on my haunches and looking wildly about," etc. Fourth, they use "carefully placed" *non sequiturs*, sabotaging "any of my managers' notions that they are 'getting somewhere'" ("somewhere" meaning "closer to the top.")

The Essential Idea:
How Power Corrupts the Mind
by Brian Resnick and National Journal

WEB LINK: https://bit.ly/3PxqOET

Resnick notes a study demonstrating that when people feel powerful, other people appear less so. Taller people tend to receive a higher salary than shorter ones.

Resnick reports on lab experiments. In one, asking someone to recall a time they felt powerful makes them feel more powerful in the present. In "the dictator game," participants are put in charge of "doling out the compensation for another participant." Dominant, expansive body positions seem to generate a feeling of power.

Resnick argues that power in itself isn't corrupting; instead, it's freeing. But once in a position of power, things manifest in different ways. For example, "the powerful are … less likely to take into account the perspective of others." Power "lends" benefits: "powerful people are more likely to take decisive action." "Power reduces awareness of constraints." "Powerful people tend to think more abstractly." Powerful people downplay risks.

Resnick reports that, in the lab, "people who are given more power ... see more choice." But Resnick adds that having power means you are "free of the punishment that one could exert upon you for the thing you did," which, the author says, paves the way for hypocrisy. Resnick referenced a study showing that powerful participants were less tolerant of cheating than the less powerful.

Resnick says that people with power "not only take what they want because they can do so unpunished, but also because they intuitively feel they are entitled to do so." Apparently "where there's hypocrisy, infidelity seems to follow." It seems that "dishonesty and power go hand in hand."

But it's not that the powerful are all bad people, Resnick says. Research indicates that when putting people in a high-powered role who have prosocial values, these people will tend to be more prosocial, "the more power they have." The more self-centered, the more selfish.

Resnick suggests that the "take away" for the "most powerful" might be to promote self-awareness. "If we realize, when in power, what it might be doing to our minds, perhaps we can correct ourselves. Perhaps."

The Essential Idea:
The Moral Mind: How We Decide

from *How We Decide*

by Jonah Lehrer

Lehrer notes that inducing a "temporary state of mind blindness," where the sympathetic areas of the brain are turned off, allows dictators to exist. However, even those with absolute power usually "remain constrained by their sympathetic instincts," except "when the dictator cannot see the responder." In other words, "once people become socially isolated, they stop stimulating the feelings of other people. Their moral intuitions are never turned on."

Another "blind spot in the sympathetic brain" is statistics: "They don't activate our moral emotions. That is why we are riveted when one child falls down a well but turn a blind eye to the millions of people who die every year for lack of clean water."

Lehrer says that the capacity for making moral decisions is innate, but "it still requires the right kind of experience in order to develop." Lehrer speculates that for some people "something goes amiss during the developmental process," and that they are "permanently damaged" by child abuse. "Cruelty makes us cruel. Abuse makes us abusive. It's a tragic loop."

But Lehrer adds that "we are designed to feel one another's pain so that we're extremely distressed when we hurt others and commit moral transgressions. Sympathy is one of humanity's most basic instincts. Evolution has programmed us to care about one another."

References

Broder, Eric. 1998. *The Below-the-Belt Manager.* New York: Warner Books.

Lehrer, Jonah. 2009. "The Moral Mind." In *How We Decide*, 187–195. Boston: Houghton Mifflin Harcourt.

Resnick, Brian, and National Journal. 2013. "How Power Corrupts the Mind." *The Atlantic*, July 9.

CHAPTER 7

Hobbled by Racism and Sexism
Perilous Pitfalls for People of Color and Women

Introduction

In meetings, all people are not invited to participate equally. For one thing, women and many minorities have historically been excluded from membership. Secondly, when they are present, there are numerous devices to sideline their participation and diminish it when offered. The same is true for other discriminated-against individuals.

Training in meeting participation is not something we go through. It is very much like the American version of peeling a banana: when I ask my students, at least three-quarters of them say they cut the stalk, while much of the world holds the banana by the stalk and scores the bottom pare (where the fibers are weaker) to start the peel. Who knows how these became the norm? But the use of traditional, and poorer, practices is powerful. In meetings, the absence of better-practice training and behavioral standards leads to the employment of traditional stereotypes and practices flourishing. Self-policing is rare, as celebrities and politicians have discovered, almost never in time. Racism, ignoring women's comments, and downright misogyny are everywhere visible. Inappropriate questions such as, "Sheila, what does the Black community think about this?" or "Susan, how do women feel (the verb of choice, as opposed to "think") about this issue?" Sarah Cooper, whose work is featured in this chapter, comments in a profile in the *Harvard Business Review* as follows:

> First, as a woman of color, I can't get away with spouting bullshit. You watch these guys in meetings have their little ways of making it look like they know what they're talking about when they don't. … Women are given all these rules—what to wear, how to sound, how much to smile, how many exclamation points to use—while men, for the most part, don't need to think about such things.

Our articles consider: Do Black people advance quicker the less Black they appear? One article examines some of the complexities of "working from home while Black." Gender parity is made more difficult because meeting styles do not currently encourage women to contribute, and a further article discusses the complexities of "speaking while female." Many of the articles highlight how men continue to dominate the public partic-ipation process, and one article considers why so many incompetent men become leaders. Another article considers one difference between men and women using Zoom for meetings, and overviews of two humorous books advise women on how to succeed in meetings.

The Essential Idea:
Being Black—but Not Too Black—in the Workplace
by *Adia Harvey Winfield*

WEB LINK: https://bit.ly/3PCjOGL

Wingfield states, "To be a Black professional is often to be alone." She suggests that Black people in medicine, law, and journalism, professions that require specialized training, often work in environments where they are in the racial minority.

Legal scholars Gulati and Carbado note that Black people do not want to be perceived as stereotypically Black. They tread cautiously so as not to upset their majority White person office. An example would be how one Black woman might chemically straighten her hair to fit in with her work counterparts as opposed to the Black woman who wears dreadlocks to work. This can be true for Latina workers as well.

People of color may advance quicker and further at work if they lose their accent. Should we be looking at creating more diverse working environments to create better workplaces for the minority professionals that are in these jobs? Wingfield says yes.

The Essential Idea: Working from Home While Black
by Laura Morgan Roberts and Courtney L. McCluney

WEB LINK: https://hbr.org/2020/06/working-from-home-while-black

Roberts and McCluney note that an increase in remote meetings (in response to the coronavirus pandemic) "poses unique authenticity challenges for the relatively small segment of Black people in the U.S.," including code-switching (adjusting speech, appearance, and behavior) "to optimize the comfort of others with the hopes of receiving fair treatment, quality service, and opportunities," and the "broadcasting" of their identities from "personal living spaces." This means that "workers are now sending social class (i.e., size of workspace) and cultural signals (i.e., furnishings, artwork) about their identity affiliations to professional colleagues and clients." Roberts and McCluney say that this "invasion of personal space increases Black workers' vulnerability to biases and judgments of their professionalism."

The authors offer three recommendations to managers and coworkers to help enact "inclusive practices in support of Black workers," including (1) welcoming and respecting boundaries (scheduling meetings in advance, encouraging contributions by phone or email, starting and ending meetings promptly, allowing cameras to be turned off, or allowing virtual backgrounds); (2) monitoring implicit biases ("against social class and cultural signals they may observe in Black employees' personal appearance and workspace"); and (3) adjusting expectations for participation (by "recognizing that people aren't working from home in a typical state of operations" and to not make assumptions about external factors).

The Essential Idea:
Seen but Rarely Heard: Why Gender Parity Is Not Equal to Gender Equality
by Stockholm Resilience Centre

WEB LINK: https://bit.ly/3uUlVxO

This piece looks at why women are not only excluded from decision-making in meetings but also why they say nothing when they are finally invited to contribute to the conversation. Women seem able to engage in "robust discussions and debate" when only women take part. Add the men, and crickets. This is true worldwide as illustrated in the Solomon Islands as well as in Rwanda, according to Michelle Dyer, center researcher.

Their study measures women's participation in public political processes. The goal is to "achieve gender equality and empower all women and girls." To do this, perhaps we should change the meeting styles to encourage women to contribute. Dyer states, "At the very least, the idea is to be aware that even though you have 50% women at a meeting there may be all these reasons why they will not contribute, and mostly it's not because they have nothing to say."

The Essential Idea:
Speaking While Female
by Sheryl Sandberg and Adam Grant

Sandberg and Grant state that when women raise an idea at a meeting, they are often interrupted, and a man may take their idea and "run with it" before the woman gets a chance to finish her thought. The man is congratulated on a fantastic idea, and the woman sits fuming. Even powerful women sit back afraid of being accused of talking too much or being aggressive, and, as a result, of being disliked. Apparently, research shows they are often right.

In the TV series "The Shield," Glen Mazzara found a way of getting his female writers to speak up by initiating a "no interruption rule" while anyone, of any gender, was speaking. It seemed to have worked. Mazzara found it made his entire team more effective.

History tells us that women who speak up are said to have to walk a tightrope at meetings, so, as a result, women often decide that "saying less is more." Sandberg and Grant are hopeful that while speaking as a women is still difficult, offering women "Obama-style meetings" (offering them the floor to speak whenever possible) will have women "leaning in" to speak up.

The Essential Idea: This Data Shows Who Grabs the Mic at Public Meetings
by Jared Brey

WEB LINK: https://rb.gy/fhao4c

Affordable housing projects are often squelched by mostly White, well-off homeowners. According to Boston University researchers, and in 100 Greater Boston cities, public meetings were made up of 95% White participants, while White people only make up 80% of the population. Latinx people make up 8% of the population but had only 1% representation at meetings. Same situation for Black people—4% of the population and 2% representation at public meetings.

Another study from BU found that public meeting participants tended to be more opposed to new development than the community as a whole. The "Not In My Back Yard" or NIMBY's, as they are commonly referred to, tend to be older, Whiter, and wealthier than their typical neighbors.

The public participation process still favors the privileged class, trying to protect their assets. The hope is that these studies provide enough evidence for policymakers to make public participation in development more democratic and to give all residents a chance to be heard.

The Essential Idea: Why Do So Many Incompetent Men Become Leaders?
by Tomas Chamorro-Premuzic

WEB LINK: https://hbr.org/2013/08/why-do-so-many-incompetent-men

This is a fascinating look at why this keeps happening over and over. Men and women differ on the reasons, but Dr. Tomas believes the main reason so many incompetent men become leaders is our inability to discern between confidence and competence. In general, people mistake confidence as a sign of competence. We are fooled into believing that men are better leaders than woman. It is believed that charisma or charm are commonly mistaken for leadership potential, and those traits are embodied more in men than in women.

Look at personality disorders such as narcissism (think Vladimir Putin). Many leaders embody these type of behavior characteristics. Dr. Tomas states that "most leaders—whether in politics or business—fail. Good leadership has always been the exception, not the norm." Sad but true.

There is now compelling evidence that women are more likely to adopt more effective leadership strategies than men. Women can set aside their selfish agendas to work for the common good of the group. Women outperform men in emotional intelligence and humility, good qualities to have when performing managerial and leadership tasks. Data suggests from thousands of managers that men are consistently more arrogant, manipulative, and risk-prone than women.

So why not more women leaders? Among other reasons, the article suggests the lack of career obstacles for incompetent men. … keeping them ever flowing to the top of the food chain.

The Essential Idea: Why Zoom Reflections Are a Feminist Issue

by Grace Tucker

WEB LINK: https://bit.ly/3Pdnak3

In this piece published in *The Michigan Daily,* the University Michigan student newspaper, Tucker examines how women, in particular, are faring in this "Zoom" epidemic of virtual classrooms. Women have always been more conscious of their appearance, way more so than their male counterparts. Whether they are in dressing rooms or locker rooms, women are often comparing their looks and bodies to their female peers.

So how does this affect women during the unprecedented time of several hours a day of virtual classes when they are on a screen? According to students interviewed, they primp more before class, sit up straight when they notice they are slouching, and generally drive themselves nuts with "habitual body monitoring."

Psychologists discuss that what drives this behavior by women seems to be deeply embedded in the subconscious. They call this "objectification theory that proposes women tend to internalize a third-person perspective—an observers' perspective—as the principal view of their physical bodies." Tucker states, "Call it what it is: Sexism that endures and a true feminist issue."

The Essential Idea:
How to Be Successful Without Hurting Men's Feelings: Nonthreatening Leadership Strategies for Women
by Sarah Cooper

Cooper takes a somewhat humorous look at the way women dodge minefields in their workplace today. They suggest, "A man's ego must be protected at all cost." Cooper tells the story of how Mary had corrected her co-worker who was driving, Steve, when his headlights were not on in the car he was driving to a company offsite. (Maybe they were going to Abilene, and no one was in agreement). Anyway, Steve laughed and turned them on. On the ride home, the same issue occurred, and this time there were other co-workers in the car. Mary hesitated to remind him again about the headlights but thought she needed to for the safety of all in the car. Mary told Steve to turn on his headlights, the other co-workers laughed, and Steve became flustered. He then became embarrassed, ran a stop sign, and T-boned an SUV. Everyone survived, but guess who every-one blamed for causing the accident? You guessed it, Mary. Co-workers thought she was telling him how to drive. Mary believed she did the right thing. Cooper believes she did the very **wrong** thing. She states, "If you have the choice between saving a man's ego or saving his life, trust me. Save his ego. He'll thank you for it later. I mean, he won't because he'll be dead, but you know what I mean."

Cooper's book addresses nonthreatening leadership strategies for women. They provide examples on how to say certain things in both a "threatening" and "nonthreatening" way. There is also an exercise and worksheet on "What I should've said." Cooper discusses how some women have a "secret power" of nonthreatening leadership. I believe women would sure like to know that secret.

The chapter on negotiation and gaslighting for beginners is interesting. Gaslighting is a form of negotiation where people make you think you are crazy, so you will become confused and unsure of yourself and ultimately agree with whatever they're saying. This has undoubtedly happened to you, and you don't even know it. Check out the movie *Gaslight*, a 1944 psychological thriller with Ingrid Bergman, from which the term originated and for how it is done.

In the book *Dare Mighty Things*, Halee Gray Scott identified the Catch-22 for all female leaders: "To succeed, you need to be liked, but to be liked, you need to temper your success." The day will come when you won't care about being either, and that's the day you will be the most successful, at least to yourself.

The Essential Idea:
100 Tricks to Appear Smart in Meetings
by Sarah Cooper

This book is a humorous look through a woman's eyes on how to conduct oneself in every type of meeting. It is complete with illustrated tips, examples, and scenarios to sound smart. Cooper presents a tongue-in-cheek approach for women to perhaps look at themselves and decide whether some of these nuggets provide any value. (Or not).

Chapters include, among others:

- **"Conference Room Playbook"**—Everything from entering the room, to where you will sit, to owning the room, and to eventually leaving the room.

- **"General Meetings—10 Key Strategies for Appearing Smart"**—With tips such as Drawing a Venn Diagram, repeating the last thing the engineer said but very, very slowly, asking, "Will this scale" (no matter what it is), step out for an important phone call, to name a few.
- **"Leaning All the Way In"**—When attending male-dominated workplace meetings, use sports metaphors (if someone did a good job, say it was a home run), learn how to talk about cars, (Tesla. com, Ferrari.com), or simply quote such movies as *The Big Lebowski*, *Animal House*, or the like.
- **"Emotional Intelligence Plan"**—Making the right faces at the right time. This one is tricky, illustrations included. At networking events, what to do with your hands, activities suggested. When out socially for cocktails, look your colleague in the eye and say cheers in a foreign language (Kanpai!).
- **"Meeting Speak Cheat Sheet"**—A guide to letting you know what is really meant by "let's table that" (That's the dumbest thing I've ever heard), "to your point earlier" (I'm kissing your backside), "let's streamline this process" (Let's keep talking about this **forever**).
- **"Famous Meetings through History"**—The Pyramids, 2630 BC; The Last Supper, Wednesday, April 1, 33 AD (original hump-day dinner); and the "Women's Suffrage Movement, 1756, when Lydia Taft is allowed to vote in a town meeting, the first victory for women in meetings. BUT remember, women should still agree with everything and be beautiful.

So, there you have it. It seems to me that these 100 tips may show engagement in the meeting but not necessarily intelligence. The intelligent woman would find a way out of attending the "painful, useless, or soul-crushing" meeting in the first place.

References

Beard, Alison. 2002. "Life's Work: An Interview with Sarah Cooper." *Harvard Business Review*, March–April.

Brey, Jared. 2018. "This (sic) Data Shows Who Grabs the Mic at Public Meetings." *NextCity*, September 6.

Chamorro-Premuzic, Tomas. 2013. "Why Do So Many Incompetent Men Become Leaders?" *Leadership*, an HBR email newsletter, August 22.

Cooper Sarah. 2016. *100 Tricks to Appear Smart in Meetings*. Kansas City, MO: Andrews McMeel Publishing.

———. 2018. *How to Be Successful Without Hurting Men's Feelings: Non-Threatening Leadership Strategies for Women*. Kansas City: MO: Andrews McMeel Publishing.

Roberts, Laura Morgan, and Courtney L. McCluney. 2020. "Working from Home While Black." *Harvard Business Review*, June 17.

Sandberg, Sheryl, and Adam Grant. 2015. "Speaking While Female." *New York Times*, January 12.

Stockholm Resistance. "Seen but Rarely Heard: Why Gender Parity Is Not Equal to Gender Equality." https://www.stockholmresilience.org/research/research-news/2018-03-05-seen-but-hardly-heard.html.

Tucker, Grace. 2020. "Why Zoom Reflections Are a Feminist Issue." *The Michigan Daily*, September 14.

Wingfield, Adia Harvey. 2015. "Being Black—but Not Too Black—in the Workplace." *The Atlantic*, October 14.

PART III

Coping Strategies for Meetings

"I know it's awkward with me being the new boss and all ...
but when you meet me in the halls,
don't act like I'm going to eat you alive."

Τhe combination of the universality and opprobrium of meetings leaves participants in a quandary. How can we cope with the fire this time and avoid the fire next time? And the time after that??

CREDIT
IMG III.1: Copyright © 2016 Depositphotos/andrewgenn.

CHAPTER 8

"Stayin' Alive" in the Meeting

Introduction

Given the problems in meetings, how does one cope? Perhaps the first option is to simply not go. But then the boss makes it mandatory. Trapped as you are, you must do something to keep yourself from the embarrassment of nodding off. So, one might try to participate, and the boss says, "When I want an idea, I will give you one!" That leads to all agreeing in public what they privately think, from "We will become the laughingstock of the business world" to "I have got to take extra medication." Sometimes, groups just agree with the boss when they privately do the opposite. Other times, participants will descend to meaningless jargon and clichés, emphasizing their meaninglessness with words like "I strongly believe" and "I am mostly in, but there is this one thing …" Still others draw on their college experiences with narcoleptic profs and pull out their old pair of "student eyeballs"—contact paper eyeballs that glue to the back of your eyelids. Then, you can appear awake while sleeping. Some few actually try to use the experience as something of a learning opportunity.

Among our articles, one discusses Irving Janis's groupthink, which has become a "catch-all term to refer to any ill-conceived group plan." This is followed by a humorous "jargon generator" and then two versions of "meetings bingo." The last article describes how to use bad meetings as a learning opportunity.

The Essential Idea:
A First Look at Communication Theory
by Emory Griffin

A section of Griffin's book on communication theory discusses Irving Janis's version of groupthink (a parallel to George Orwell's "doublethink" from *1984*), and how it caught on as a "catch-all term to refer to any ill-conceived group plan." Janis defines the occurrence of groupthink as where "concurrence-seeking" tends to override "realistic appraisal of alternative courses of action." Griffin examines Janis's eight "symptoms," and then illustrates them as examples from the Space Shuttle *Challenger* disaster.

The first two "stem from overconfidence in the group's prowess": the illusion of invulnerability and a belief in the inherent morality of the group. The next pair "reflect the tunnel vision members use to view the problem": collective rationalization and out-group stereotypes (looking "down" on outsiders). The final four "are signs of strong conformity pressure within the group": self-censorship, the illusion of unanimity, direct pressure on dissenters, and the desire to "protect a leader from assault by troublesome ideas."

Griffin notes that "in later extensions of his theory, Janis emphasized that not all bad decisions are the result of groupthink, and not all cases of groupthink end up failing."

The Essential Idea:
Jargon Generator
by Arthur Gernand

Gernand humorously suggests that "bureaucrats, educators, and others" come up with their "terminology" by using a "jargon generator," which, he says, was dreamed up by an anonymous high school administrator. The "tool" consists of two columns of "multisyllabic adjectives, then a third column of ambiguous nouns "that defy definition." Pick an adjective from each column and then a noun. For example: "integrated management outputs."

Gernand suggests using the jargon generator "when you really have nothing to say" and it will "result in absolutely no one knowing what you're talking about." But what really matters is "that (1) they will never admit it and (2) they will accept you as a decisive thinker who possesses great ability to verbalize complex ideas."

The Essential Idea:
Bullshit Buzzword Bingo
by Graham F. Scott

WEB LINK: https://www.buzzwordbingogame.com/cards/bullshit/

This humorous bingo variant "calls out some of the misguided notions, boneheaded beliefs and even downright lies that steer companies off course" by using some of the business world's "most overused clichés, buzzwords and empty jargon." Each bingo card is "randomly generated" and is suggested for use during "your next interminable conference call or meeting."

The Essential Idea:
Business Meeting Bingo
by Anonymous

WEB LINK: http://www.tysknews.com/LiteStuff/bingo.htm

This humorous bingo variant is designed to help keep you from "falling asleep in meetings and seminars" or on "long and boring conference calls." Twenty-five overused words or phrases (such as "synergy" and "strategic fit") can be written into a standard bingo 5-by-5 block. Then, "check off the appropriate block when you hear one of these words/phrases." When you get five in a row, the further suggestion is to stand and shout "Bull-shit!" instead of "Bingo!"

The Essential Idea:
From Lemons to Lemonade: Using Bad Meetings as a Learning Opportunity
by Carolyn Gier

Many of us have endured the soul-crushing experience of weekly or monthly sales meetings. Carolyn Gier tells a story of her early days as a "professional sales representative" for Pfizer and how she turned bad meetings into a learning tool, effectively turning lemons into lemonade.

The monthly sales meetings were like "status arenas," where the district manager "would call out those whose territories were doing well, and congratulate the salespeople (all men all the time, 1979). This was followed by some "wise-cracking and joke-telling" and then some "good ole boy" bantering on the part of the group that was not doing well. Carolyn inherited a poorly performing sales territory. She was determined to bring up the numbers. So, she **listened**, particularly to the salespeople who were most successful. "They were working smart," Carolyn said, "and I was listening. I also listened to what did not work in the field." "Personalities that were irritating to me in the meeting room were most likely irritating to the physicians we were trying to sell to." She learned how to be assertive without being pushy. She learned how to "get in front of the physician" to get a chance to promote Pfizer products by being disarmingly friendly to the office staff, bringing them lunch, promotional products, or whatever made their day.

Carolyn reports that "about six months into my sales career my sales numbers were at the top of the region." Everyone in management with Pfizer was happy, and those Detroit salespeople were now listening to her.

Never underestimate the art of effective listening. That's taking a lemon and turning it into lemonade.

References

Anonymous. "Business Meeting Bingo." http://www.tysknews.com/LiteStuff/bingo.htm.

Gernand, Arthur. 1984. "Jargon Generator." *The Wilson Quarterly,* 8[2], Spring, 170–171.

Gier, Carolyn. 2022. "From Lemons to Lemonade: Using Bad Meetings as a Learning Opportunity." In Tropman, John, with Daniel Madaj and Carolyn Gier, *Fixing Broken Meetings: A Manual on Meeting Rotten-ocity, Deleterious Decisions, and Ineffective Implementation.* San Diego, CA: Cognella. (This article was written especially for this book.)

Griffin, Emory. 1991. *A First Look at Communication Theory.* New York: McGraw-Hill, 235–246.

Scott, Graham F. 2015. "Bullshit Bingo." *Canadian Business,* Mar 4. https://www.buzzwordbingogame.com/cards/bullshit/.

PART IV

To Decide or Not to Decide, That Is the Question

"What if we don't change at all ...
and something magical just happens."

High-quality decisions are usually not on the mind of meeting participants. They are either anxious because the decisional challenge is great and the skills available in the room are not up to the task, or the challenge is below their pay grade and they are bored. So, they employ one or more of the four Ds—Delay, Defer, Deflect, Deny—to avoid deciding at all. One group I worked with was a very large C-level group that never could decide anything. Working with the group to systematize its agenda (which was always the same—old business, new business, and with no topics, either). We created a timed-drive meeting structure. If a decision could not be made within the allotted time, we would put it on "the list" and return to it in the next meeting. For about a month, I was a hero. Then I was fired. "The list" was 60 items long. It turned out that they thought putting an item on "the list" WAS the decision. And this was a six-billion-dollar company. The following chapter details some examples of the Four Ds in action.

CREDIT

CHAPTER 9

Decision Avoidance Psychosis

Introduction

Groupthink, mentioned in the previous chapter, is a popular mode of decision avoidance. While "not to decide is to decide" is a true statement, most people do not see it, or feel it, that way.

Decision avoidance is one of the approaches to decision-building. "This too shall pass" is one of the ways that one can avoid confronting "the painful necessity of choice." There is substantial literature on the pain of choice (see References at the end of this chapter for one suggestion). One famous novel, *Crime and Punishment*, seems to be mostly about the pain of choice, a small part in the middle where a choice is enacted, and then the remainder of the time spent in regret of choice. Buyer's remorse is another popular phrase that talks about the regret of choice. The fact that half of marriages end in divorce affirms that we are not that good at choice (or perhaps it is making choices work). But there are other widely known examples. America's infrastructure (roads, bridges, and dams) is widely known to be falling apart. Governments at all levels have played "kick the can down the road" (also known as "fixing the infrastructure.") "That is a great idea! Let's not do that!"

There is a lake in Oregon that hosts thousands and thousands of migratory birds. It is in danger of drying up because the aquifer has been drained by farmers over the years. This is not a new problem, but a well-known one (Cook 2022). Apparently, the threat of aquatic and horrific avian fatalities is insufficient to take action. These last two examples illustrate a common feature of decision avoidance psychosis. Where problems involve multiple organizational units and interests, they need to be managed, not exactly "solved." So, it is easy for projects to fall between the cracks. Strong leadership, the sort Dwight Eisenhower showed in the interstate road initiative and the sort Robert Moses showed in New York State, is needed and missing.

Our articles cover the tendency to reward the behavior we mean to discourage, provide a showcase of the "psychology of doing nothing," and look at why we avoid making decisions. There is a five-step process to improving decision-making in meetings, and there are a few examples from a guide to "saving your good idea from getting shot down."

The Essential Idea: On the Folly of Rewarding A, While Hoping for B

by Steven Kerr

WEB LINK: https://bit.ly/3IstqSo

Kerr says that "numerous examples exist of reward systems that are fouled up in that the types of behavior rewarded are those which the rewarder is trying to discourage, while the behavior desired is not being rewarded at all," and then gives examples from politics, war, universities, consulting, sports, government, and business. A table of common management reward follies includes such things as looking for teamwork but rewarding individual effort, committing to quality and candor but rewarding "shipping on schedule," and agreeing with the boss.

Kerr suggests four general factors that "may be pertinent to an explanation of why fouled-up reward systems seem to be so prevalent": fascination with an "objective," over-emphasis on highly visible behaviors, hypocrisy, and emphasis on morality or equity rather than efficiency.

Kerr recommends altering "the reward system," noting that sometimes the reward systems installed "are paying off for behavior" other than what is being sought. Kerr suggested exploring what types of behavior are currently being rewarded and to make sure that "the formal reward system … positively reinforces desirable behavior and does not constitute an obstacle to be overcome."

The Essential Idea:
The Psychology of Doing Nothing: Forms of Decision Avoidance Resulting from Reason and Emotion
by Christopher J. Anderson

Anderson says that "in understanding decisions not to act," instead of "trying to reconcile regret and actual human behavior with a rational scheme … psychologists should instead be investigating the 'why' behind emotional influences on behavior …" Anderson says that understanding decision avoidance is "one step toward placing emotions in context … including its functionality."

While Anderson notes that the experience of postponing and avoiding certain choices is universal, it often appears to work against individuals' goals. "Delays transform into lost opportunities, and adhering to the status quo is frequently unjustified given advantageous alternatives. Still, individuals persist in seeking default no-action, no-change options."

Decision avoidance has not been studied "in an integrated manner" because it does not fit neatly into the current paradigms in clinical, cognitive, or social psychology. "Almost everyone can cite examples of the high price of a failure to act, and there is evidence that humans are only becoming more indecisive."

Anderson examines two principles that may help explain who "humans so frequently engage in decision avoidance": conservation of energy (avoidant, inactive behavior occurring "simply because the decision-maker does not recognize that an opportunity has presented itself or that there is a need to make a decision") and multiple causation ("an antecedent of decision avoidance," because "a complex and common behavior … may have more than one cause").

Decision avoidance phenomena include status quo and omission biases (a preference for "no change in the state of the world"), choice deferral ("taking time to search for better alternatives"), and inaction inertia ("a reluctance to take action").

Anderson mention 10 factors that can act "to increase or decrease one's anticipated feelings of regret," including reversibility (a decision's outcome is reversible), expected outcome feedback ("anticipated regret"), degree of loss aversion ("the human tendency to weight outcomes viewed as losses … more heavily than equivalent gains"), and perceived responsibility (regret is anticipated when one is perceived to be personally responsible for the outcome).

Anderson notes 15 contributors to selection difficulty, including decision strategy (such as between "compensatory and noncompensatory decision rules"), reasons (decision justifications), preference uncertainty (being unsure of which options best meet the goals), and degree of structure (the less structure and definition, the more difficult).

The Essential Idea:
Stop the Meeting Madness
by Leslie A. Perlow

Perlow notes that poking fun at meetings is "the stuff of *Dilbert* cartoons—we can all joke about how soul-sucking and painful they are. But that pain has real consequences for teams and organizations."

Perlow says that most of what has been written about this problem usually take the form of discrete solutions: "Establish a clear agenda, hold your meeting standing up, delegate someone to attend in your place, and so on." Perlow says that real improvement "requires systemic change, because meetings affect how people collaborate and how they get their own work done."

"Time is zero-sum," Perlow says. "Every minute spent in a wasteful meeting eats into time for solo work that's equally essential for creativity and efficiency." Also, schedules riddled with meetings "interrupt 'deep work'" (the ability to focus without distraction on a cognitively demanding task).

Perlow says it is possible to change the way your team and your organization approach meetings. He describes a five-step process: Collect data from each person; interpret the data together; agree on a collective, personally relevant goal; set milestones and monitor progress; and regularly debrief as a group.

Perlow notes that "problems ensue when meetings are scheduled and run without regard to their impact on both group and solo work time. Often, groups end up sacrificing collective or individual needs— or both—by default." Perlow says that many organizations "endure the triple whammy of meetings that are (1) too frequent, (2) poorly timed, and (3) badly run, leading to losses in productivity, collaboration, and well-being for both groups and individuals."

Perlow says that "altering something as basic as meetings can have far-reaching implications. Meetings do not have to be a trap; they can be a conduit for change." Meetings "can improve productivity, communication, and integration of the team's work."

The Essential Idea:
Buy-In: Saving Your Good Idea from Getting Shot Down

By John P. Kotter and Lorne A. Whitehead

Kotter and Whitehead's book notes that good ideas are often stymied and then eventually killed by "confounding questions, inane comments, and verbal bullets—either directly at you or, even worse, behind your back."

They not only list 24 "idea killers," but they give possible responses. For example, when someone says, "We've been successful, why change?" a response could be to note that "those who fail to adapt eventually become extinct." Or when someone says, "What about this, and that, and that (etc.)?" a response could be that "all good ideas, if they are new, raise dozens of questions that cannot be answered with certainty." Or when someone says, "If this was such a great idea, why hasn't it been done already?" a response could be that there is a first time for everything.

References

Anderson, Christopher J. 2003. "The Psychology of Doing Nothing: Forms of Decision Avoidance Result from Reason and Emotion." *Psychological Bulletin* 129 (1), February.

Cook, Emily Cureton. 2022. "It's Feared a Vital Lake in Oregon Could Run Dry Within a Generation." *Oregon Public Broadcasting*, April 4. https://bit.ly/3vPxqaS.

Kerr, Steven. 1995. "On the Folly of Rewarding A While Hoping for B." *The Academy of Management Executive*, 9, 1, February

Kotter, John P., and Lorne A. Whitehead. 2010. *Buy-In: Saving Your Good Idea from Getting Shot Down*. Boston: Harvard Business School Press.

Perlow, Leslie A., Constance Noonan Hadley, and Eunice Eun, "Stop the Meeting Madness." (A version of this article appeared in the July–August 2017 issue of *Harvard Business Review*, 62–69).

United Way of America, 1974. *The Painful Necessity of Choice*.

PART V

Decision Debacles, Drift, Difficulties, Delays, and Disruptions

"My last comment 'appeared' to be inviting feedback.
Do not be fooled."

As the Meeting Masters Research projects began to explore findings, some new problems emerged. Good meetings did not always produce high-quality decisions, any more than good ingredients can produce a quality meal. Good meetings seem to be the *sine qua non* of good decisions, but sometimes just having a good meeting **becomes** the goal rather than the means to the accomplishment of a decision.

Since decisions tear at the fabric of group cohesion, it is imperative that these resistance forces be overcome. Often, they are not, leading to bad decisions (debacles). Sometimes, meeting leaders cannot "close." Sometimes, the group experiences "conceptual collapse" and has no idea what to do and drifts into a delay. For example, one colleague we worked with always made the same disruptive contribution, "I think we need more research on this issue." This was almost always a showstopper. Understanding what is involved in decision-building becomes key to successful decision-building. Some of the Meeting Masters were also Decision Maestros.

CHAPTER 10

Decision Rotten-ocity and Partialization

Introduction

There is a lot written about rotten decisions. Russia's incursion into Ukraine in 2022 is a perfect example. But the US has had its experiences with similar decisions, such as the oppression of the Native American Community, other racism, suppression of women, the Civil War, and at least three other wars—Vietnam, Iraq, and Afghanistan. Sometimes exhaustion sets in and participants cave in. They settle for poor, low-quality decisions. And that does not include historical boners by the Supreme Court, such as *Plessy v. Ferguson* (which legitimated "separate but equal schools"), which was overturned by *Brown v. Board of Education,* and the 2022 overturning of *Roe v. Wade.*

How these come about is less clear. Frequently it is because decision makers see others as they see themselves, creating a conceptual vacuum. Other times it arises as a result of a) a toxic person and b) failure to control that person. Participants give up. They just cannot stand it. If that person is the boss, one might also experience intimidation.

Our articles examine a variety of rotten decisions and include three signs that you're the toxic person and eight stupid mistakes that even smart people make.

The Essential Idea:
A Sampler of Rotten Decisions
by John E. Tropman

"It seemed like a good idea at the time" is maybe a subtle way of saying, "I chose poorly." Tropman discusses the equation, "Results = Decision + Implementation" with adding or subtracting luck for possibly a more realistic outcome of the decision. Good Decisions are sometimes very elusive indeed.

Tropman examines Folly, Group Think, and a personal favorite, the Abilene Paradox. In the Abilene Paradox, the group comes to a decision that NO ONE wants while thinking everyone else wants it. Therefore, in the end, not a single person gets what they want.

Of course, there are always "off-limits" discussions of problems. This is where we do not want to discuss a problem, and we won't even discuss why we are not discussing it. That pot will boil over eventually, and everyone better run for cover when it does.

The Essential Idea:
3 Signs You're the Toxic Person in Your Workplace (and What to Do About It)
by John Boitnott

WEB LINK: https://rb.gy/mhy9i5

"People tend to have a natural aversion to those who make it all about themselves." Boitnott contends, "almost every workplace has a least one toxic employee." Could that be you? Boitnott shares the three common traits of toxic employees.

1. **"You make everything about you."** It would seem all of us are guilty of this at some point in our lives. To counteract this, "make an effort to listen more and talk less."

2. **"You say and do passive-aggressive things."** According to Boinott, employees tend to do or say passive-aggressive things when they feel threatened, jealous, or insecure. So, how about taking a walk instead? You will release pent-up anger and will be less likely to take it out on your co-workers as a backhanded passive-aggressive remark.

3. **"You're jealous of the success of others."** You know the type, the teacher's pet. Now let's say someone else starts getting attention. "Pet" may get jealous and become a toxic presence in the office. The solution is "stop comparing yourself to others. Realize that your co-worker's success in no way diminishes your own. Redirect your jealous energy into something positive." Just think ... the possibilities are limitless to you!

The Essential Idea: 8 Stupid Mistakes That Even Smart People Make
by Travis Bradberry

Bradberry contends that "it's good to be smart. However, even the most intelligent of people have the reputation of making silly mistakes, especially in the common-sense arena." As Voltaire famously stated, "Common sense is not so common." The term "bias blind spot" refers to the notion that we are great at finding other people's mistakes but bad at seeing our own. Highly intelligent people find it hard to accept that they did make a mistake. That seems contrary to Socrates's belief that, "I know that I am intelligent, because I know that I know nothing."

Here are some of the key points why smart people fail.

1. **Smart people are overconfident**—Don't think they need help and believe no one is smart enough to help them anyway.

2. **They push too hard**—Set the bar too high for others to achieve greatness.

3. **They always need to be right**—Highly intelligent people take it as a personal attack when they are wrong.

4. **They lack emotional intelligence**—Not enough can be said about how important your EQ is. Enough said.

5. **They give up when they fail.**

6. **They fail to develop grit**.

7. **They multitask**—According to Stanford research, multitasking makes you less productive.

8. **They have a hard time accepting feedback**—Smart people believe that nobody can give them valuable feedback. Who can be smarter than they are? This leads to toxic relationships, both professionally and personally.

So, take a good, long, honest look at yourself, "Are you too smart for your own good?"

References

Beard, Alison. 2022. "Sarah Cooper, Life's Work." *Harvard Business Review*, March–April.

Boitnott, John. 2018. "3 Signs You're the Toxic Person in Your Workplace (and What to Do About It)," *Inc*.com,

Bradberry, Travis. 2016. "8 Stupid Mistakes That Even Smart People Make." *Inc.*, July 21.

Tropman, John E. "A Sampler of Rotten Decisions" (unpublished manuscript).

CHAPTER 11

Decision Circumvention

Introduction

Sometimes decisions can be put off or obfuscated. Students are often like this. They make an appointment because they need an incomplete or other help. But because of nervousness and the power differential, they wait until minute 19 of a 20-minute session to get to the key point. This strategy is an awful one because (a) it puts the decision-maker at a real disadvantage, which prompts (b) the decision to propose to defer/circumvent because of insufficient time. Since decisions are essentially plural ("What shall we have for dinner tonight?" has many parts), sometimes partializing the problem is selected, in which a small noncontroversial portion of the decision mosaic is agreed upon while leaving the more important portions for later work in the meeting.

This chapter considers four articles: one discusses the tendency of patients and clients to reveal their most important revelations in the last seconds of a session (just as they are ready to leave). In another, a discussion of the Abilene Paradox suggests making confronters into heroes. ("Instead of shooting messengers, reward them.") Then, there is a "practical guide for detecting, diagnosing, and dealing with defensive routines," and, last, a brief discourse about one of many memos from a humorous, fictitious book of meeting memos.

The Essential Idea:
Door Knob Revelations: Clients Reveal Greatest Intimacies with Hand on the Door Knob
by Loren A. Olson

Olson is an Iowa psychiatrist who, upon retiring, wrote a book, *Finally Out: Letting Go of Living Straight—A Psychiatrist's Own Story*. In his book, Olson did what so many of his patients did during their sessions with him. Dr. Olson finally revealed that he struggled with his sexual orientation for all of his life. His patients never knew this about their treating physician. Just as Olson did, patients often reveal the most important revelations about their mental health struggles during the last 30 seconds of a session just when they are ready to leave. Hence the term, "Door Knob Revelations." "Finally Out" was his.

Olson believes that you "don't help people by giving them a fish but by teaching them how to catch a fish." He has always practiced psychotherapy with two basic beliefs:

1. **Always zero in on the affect**—(mood, emotion)
2. **Always explore the resistance**—(explore why you feel you can't tell me)

The healing powers of psychotherapy come from genuine warmth, accurate empathy, and unconditional positive regard. These are qualities not everyone has. That may determine a great therapist from an average one. According to Olson, "as we get older, we must recognize that life is not about the number of toys we accumulate, but instead it is about the capacity to connect with others on a deeply human level." That is … what makes a great life.

The Essential Idea:
An Abilene Defense: Commentary One
by Rosabeth Moss Kanter

WEB LINK: http://palousemindfulness.com/docs/Abilene-Paradox.pdf, **p. 37**

In the Abilene Paradox, everyone in the group makes a decision that no one individually wants. Publicly you may agree, but in private you disagree with the decision. The result is often troublesome.

So, how do we stay out of Abilene? Kanter believes you manage communication by establishing debates. This requires a good manager who lets everyone express what they really think. "Assign gadflies, devil's advocates, fact-checkers, and second guessers." Make these assigned roles so that everyone gets a chance to play. Encourage "organizational graffiti" that allows people to comment anonymously on any issue.

Also, Kanter believes that you "make confronters into heroes. Instead of shooting messengers, reward them." This will encourage people to speak up. Develop a culture of pride within your organization, and empower your people. This doesn't necessarily mean you will stay out of Abilene, but to avoid it, you can always permit your employees to redefine their road trip.

The Essential Idea:
Dear Committee Members
by Julie Schumacher

This is a humorous, cautionary tale from someone who actually reads your plan before the dreaded meeting. They caution their boss on two considerations they may not have thought of. They lament how the group argued for weeks about a semicolon and cautions that a meeting could turn into an immediate mental health referral or a 911 call. An interesting memo, and remember, "Always think positively."

The Essential Idea: Overcoming Defensive Routines in the Workplace
by William R. Noonan

Well-meaning and smart people create vicious cycles of defensive behavior. This vicious cycle is used to protect themselves from embarrassment and threat. Defensive routines exist in all organizations.

Noonan "provides a practical guide for detecting, diagnosing, and dealing with defensive routines.

- Look beyond the parts to the interdependency among the parts.
- Re-evaluate underlying mental models.
- Think in loops.
- Address generic patterns.

We need to be able to have difficult conversations regardless of the person's problematic ego. There is a discussion of the "Unilateral Control Model, I am right and you are wrong. The sense is, things are going as I hoped and intended. Things are going my way when I feel in control. I know what I am doing. I feel competent." Of course, this is only one side to the thinking, to win, not lose.

Maps of defensive routines can be comprised of interpersonal, team, and interdivisional loops of interactions. To think in loops, you visualize a pattern of interrelationships. When they work, they can reduce the tendency to blame and provide a way to navigate through defensive behavior.

To address generic defensive routines, try Noonan's simple "STEP" exercise in turning the conversation around.

Finally, don't forget to "weed the garden." You can tolerate a certain number of weeds, but you surely don't want them to overtake your garden.

References

Kanter, Rosabeth Moss. "An Abilene Defense: Commentary One." http://palousemindfulness.com/docs/Abilene-Paradox.pdf, 37.

Noonan, William R. 2007–2008. "Overcoming Defensive Routines in the Workplace." *The Systems Thinker,* Vol. 18 No. 10, Dec./Jan.

Olson, Loren A., MD. 2011. "Door Knob Revelations." *Psychology Today* blog, October 8.

Schumacher, Julia. *Dear Committee Members.* Penguin Random House, 34–35.

References

PART VI

Some Explanations and a Cautionary Tale

Never Underestimate People's Commitment to Rotten Practices

"Here's where you give me non-comprehending nods of approval."

Perhaps we do not need to focus on this material because the prevalence of rotten meetings and terrible decisions is proof enough that most of us have deep commitments to historical practices no matter how unsatisfactory they may be. So, one conundrum that deserves attention is to seek an explanation for this persistence. A sociologist might think that some latent functions are served through and by manifest ones. Typically, when some practice appears odd or wrong, yet it persists, it is a good idea to look for some hidden functionality. So, by way of example, the "mask rebellion" involving Covid is a recent odd case that falls into this category. What might the latent function be? Perhaps it could be the formation of a publicly identifiable community of the like-minded in a time of anomie.

CHAPTER 12

Byzantine Bureaucracies

Introduction

Once a decision has been built, whether excellent or poor, it moves into a larger organization for implementation. The implementation itself involves several phases. The first is operationalizing the requirements outlined in the decision while, at the same time, identifying the staff and resources needed to provide the people and resources for those requirements. Following that, relevant individuals need to be assembled, and a plan is developed. Sometimes, the decision involves little extra work; often, though, a significant project is involved, touching numerous departments in the organization (and sometimes outside the organization). The "plan" requires leadership and administration, which is often lost, especially as an organization grows larger. Departments and individuals involved often have policy preferences that differ from the one they are implementing. That may "slow-walk" their part in the implementation or lose the request among other tactics. Or, narratively, they may be overworked or under-skilled, on vacation, out sick, or involved in many other situations that deliberately or unintentionally SNAFU the implementation.

Additionally, there may need to be a pilot developed and alpha and beta testing employed. All of these (not to mention supply chain problems, front office distractions, etc.) may lengthen the time from what the medical community calls "bench to bedside" and the auto industry (and other industries) calls "from art to part."

Our articles here include a humorous version of the "whisper" game, also known as "The Plan," and an examination of President Trump's Coronavirus Task Force, which seemed to be more about looking like someone was working on something than getting something done.

The Essential Idea:
Project Planning, Scheduling, and Control
by James P. Lewis

As in the "whisper" game, where a statement is repeated around a circle, and eventually the statement is changed almost beyond recognition, Lewis suggests a version where the desire to soften the impact of the statement can eventually end with an opposite statement. In this example, a manager went to their superior and said, "It is a crock of excrement, and none may abide the odor thereof." By the time the statement reached the president, it was "This powerful new product will promote the growth of the company."

The Essential Idea:
Trump's Coronavirus Task Force
by Alex Pareene

WEB LINK: https://rb.gy/g4dvr6

In a May 2020 article in *The New Republic*, Pareene described then-president Trump's "coronavirus task force" as a "farce." Pareene says that the task force "is the perfect model of governance for our time because it is made up of people who assign tasks to other people, wait for them to finish, and then assume that somehow, they got it done themselves."

Pareene reports that Trump began by announcing an "official task force on reopening the economy," then "upgraded" it to an "advisory committee of America's Top 200 Economic Minds," whose point was to come up with a plan to "jump-start the engine of economic prosperity once the administration got the pandemic under control." But three weeks after these announcements, "approximately nothing" had been done to get the pandemic under control.

Pareene speculates that the point of creating the task forces was "less to do difficult tasks than to assure everyone that someone was working on those tasks."

Pareene notes that almost every executive or elected official has one or more "concurrently running task forces" that give the appearance of having the situation or situations under control.

"The thing the task forces have in common is that they tend to include very few people who have had to live with the decisions made by the sort of executives and CEOs placed on these panels. The economic task forces … include … no workers."

The Essential Idea: Summary
from *Execution: The Discipline of Getting Things Done*
by Larry Bossidy and Ram Charan

Bossidy and Charan assert that "execution," by which they mean "the ability to follow your plans and get things accomplished," is not something leaders can delegate, but must be "engraved in the corporate culture." When strategies fail, they say, "you should look for the problem in poor execution."

Bossidy and Charan say that to reach any goal, "A company has to align its operations, strategy, and staff." They list the three phases of cultural change: (1) communication of what is wanted, (2) planning the change out, and (3) giving rewards to those who "perform in a way that makes the planned changes a reality." They also list three aspects of execution (it's a discipline you practice, it is every leader's primary job, it should be a "core element" of the corporate culture), and seven behaviors of good executors (including knowing your people and business, insisting on realism, and rewarding the doers). They also provide several questions to ask when assessing the company's strategy.

References

Bossidy, Larry, and Ram Charan. 2002. *Execution: The Discipline of Getting Things Done.* New York: Crown Business.

Lewis, James P. 2010. *Project Planning, Scheduling and Control.* New York: McGraw Hill.

Pareene, Alex. 2020. "Trump's Coronavirus Task Farce." *New Republic*, May 7. https://newrepublic.com/article/157642/trumps-coronavirus-task-farce.

CHAPTER 13

The Latent Function of Meaningless Meetings

Introduction

But the intriguing question remains—what is the purpose of useless meetings? One answer seems to be that they are not useless to everybody. Managers like them because, while they are called a "meeting," they are—especially the weekly staff meeting—an easy way for the manager to get briefed. So, a considerable number of "meetings" are really "briefings." A second function—mentioned before—is an opportunity for power strutting—sometimes by the manager but sometimes by other employees. Strutting is more satisfying if there is an audience. One, of course, can strut alone but that is not the point of the strut as there is no one to intimidate. A third reason is to fill in the empty spaces in the workweek. Jobs wrap up early; assignments shift; key players are absent; etc. But organizational America, with some exceptions (professors!), has workers strapped to a 9–5+ schedule, and the organization needs a "filler." These vacant interstices require "apparent" work as discussed in one of the readings from Chapter 8, "Bullsh—t Bingo." Finally, it might be a "fake meeting." A fake meeting occurs when a decision has already been made, but the boss wants to give the appearance of involvement.

Our articles in this chapter include a look at "bullshit jobs" ("pointless jobs just to keep us all working") and at "latent functions" of public dysfunctionality. Another article argues that organizations hire smart people but then encourage them "not to use their intelligence"; another wonders if salaried workers are being overworked and "for free."

The Essential Idea:
On the Phenomenon of Bullshit Jobs:
A Work Rant
by David Graeber

By 1930, John Maynard Keynes predicted that countries like Great Britain or the US would be on a 15-hour workweek. Wrong. Our technology would have improved to help us do more in less time. Wrong … instead, new technology has made us all work more. Who should we blame? Ourselves. Given the choice of working fewer hours or having more toys and pleasure, what did we choose? Of course, we chose more toys and pleasure. Welcome to America.

Graeber contends we now have what he calls "bullshit jobs." These are a kind of pointless jobs just to keep us all working. The creation of whole new industries like financial services, telemarketing, expansions of corporate law, academic and health administration, human resources, and public relations have grown immensely. People are working so much in their 9–5 jobs that ancillary jobs have developed like "dog walkers, delivery people for Amazon, Door-Dash, and the like."

Graeber believes that this is not an economic issue but a moral and political one. "The ruling class has figured out that a happy and productive population with free time on their hands is a mortal danger." Something like, as in Proverbs 16, "Idle hands are the devil's workshop."

Now, some of us believe that we are making a meaningful contribution to the world. For that, you should be proud. You may not be paid much, but, hey, at least you love your work. Graeber believes that "the more one's work benefits other people, the less you are likely to be paid for it." Calling all social workers.

The Essential Idea: On the Latent Functions of Apparently Dysfunctional Practices
by John E. Tropman

Tropman spent a career researching meeting excellence and its components. He states, "Never underestimate people's commitment to rotten practices!" Such problematic practices as absent agendas, unequal participation, " the eating meeting," waiting for no-shows, big talkers … the list goes on.

Tropman believes that public dysfunctionality is so widespread that there must be some latent functionality running below the surface. What else is going on?

According to Tropman, several elements of latent functionality emerged:

- **Absorb Empty Time:** Meetings provide the appearance of work and fill holes in the workday schedule.
- **Control of Staff:** Monday am and Friday pm meetings are usually set to control your staff.
- **Power Display**: Meetings allow supervisors and managers an occasion to display and exercise their power.

Other points mentioned include the illusion of participation, the fake meeting, the report meeting, and taking comfort in the routine of the organizational ritual.

Therefore, the dysfunction continues because the latent functionality serves a variety of purposes … Horror of horrors, is it us?

The Essential Idea: Stupefied: How Organizations Enshrine Collective Stupidity, and Employees Are Rewarded for Checking Their Brains at the Office Door
by André Spicer

Every year the new best and brightest graduates emerge from their four-year colleges and graduate schools excited for their future and putting their superior intelligence to work. Spicer contends they are in for a bit of a surprise. Instead of using the intelligence they were selected for, they are not expected to use it. If they happen to want to use their intelligence, it will be met with dismay from their colleagues and bosses. What's a young upstart to do?

Organizations like to hire smart people but then encourage their new hires not to use their intelligence. Rather, a young upstart should turn off those brains and focus on getting things done.

Spicer discusses the power of "the brand." He uses the fatal attempt by British Airways to rebrand "The world's favorite airline" by replacing the Union Jack flag on the plane's tail fins with "World Art" designs. The change was disastrous, and British Airways reverted back to its old tail fin (with its tail between its legs) and millions of dollars lost.

Another Spicer analysis found that US companies pay above-average salaries to top appointees in hopes of attracting above-average candidates. The high pay did not impact the company's performance. All it did was ratchet up the senior executives' pay. Think of GM, affectionately known in the Detroit area as "Generous Motors" and their filing of bankruptcy to bring that point home.

Spicer states, "There are times when it's impossible to hide the rotten fruits of the collective stupidity." There is a downside to being relentlessly positive. If no one speaks up for fear of being a naysayer, then reality is lost. (Similar to Vladimir Putin and the Soviet generals.)

The last piece of advice is to keep moving. Do not let your mistakes catch up with you. We have all been warned, or, as the Queen of Hearts said, "off with their heads.")

The Essential Idea: A Life of Hard Labor: Capitalism and Working Hours: The Salaried Laborer's Free Hours

from *The Overworked American: The Unexpected Decline of Leisure*
by Juliet B. Schor

Salary or hourly, which is the better way to be paid? According to Schor, salary employment increased substantially in the twentieth century. She found that 40% of all US employees are paid by salary. In 2020, this increased to 45%. But what about the extra hours that are almost surely expected by employers of salaried workers? Well, you work those for free.

Schor laments that many workers cannot escape long hours and remain successful on the job. Employers expect more than 9-5, and they want weekends and nights, too. If you don't, you may be passed over for promotions because maybe you don't have the "right attitude."

Look at what happened in 2022. With the use of cell phones, computers, Covid, and working from home, the "changing of the job" has been immense. As more and more salaried workers are working from home and in different global time zones, are American workers expected to be on call 12 or more hours a day? The work-from-home concept has really caught on since Covid hit. It seems people like the flexibility of hours, the gain of commuting time, no dress-up for work, etc. But still, I have to wonder, what would you pay me to work hourly? And what about overtime pay? I might be better off as it seems I am always taking a call on what was once my free time.

References

Graber, David. 2013. "On the Phenomenon of Bullshit Jobs." *Strike!*, August.

Pareene, Alex. 2020. "Trump's Coronavirus Task Farce." *The New Republic*, May 7. https://newrepublic.com/article/157642/trumps-coronavirus-task-farce.

Schor, Juliet B. 1992. "A Life of Hard Labor: Capitalism and Working Hours: The Salaried Laborer's Free Hours." In *The Overworked American: The Unexpected Decline of Leisure*. New York: Basic Books, Chapter 3, pp. 43–83.

Spicer, André. 2016. "Stupefied: How organizations enshrine collective stupidity and employees are rewarded for checking their brains at the office door." *Aeon*, September 27.

Tropman, John E. "On the Latent Functions of Apparently Dysfunctional Practices" (unpublished) manuscript).

PART VII

Meetings Remedies

"There's a bit of disconnect
with your leadership style."

One would think that as problematic processes and ineffective interventions are observed, relevant participants and systems would take action. One would think. But that thought would be wrong. That thought is all too rarely acted upon. Bad meetings and poor decisions are sustained by bad press, which, in turn, is sustained by a self-fulfilling prophecy. Participants do not prepare for meetings or build careful decisions. As a result, things go badly. That "badly" then becomes evident when there is no point in improved preparation or careful examination of "what went wrong" but, rather, evokes a hapless shrug and a divisive quip, such as "Well, everyone knows that meetings take minutes to waste hours."

To this general conundrum, we can add that there is not a lot of research on meetings. The literature available is largely anecdotal. However, Google has done some excellent work on successful teams—a two-year study (not exactly meetings, but very close)—with psychological safety as the key ingredient. It also has excellent software that aids in meeting preparation and the display of meeting materials. But Google, unlike many places, is interested.

A graphic from *re:Work* shows five steps toward a healthy workplace: (1) psychological safety (team members feel safe to take risks and be vulnerable in front of each other), (2) dependability (team members get things done on time and meet Google's high bar for excellence), (3) structure and clarity (team members have clear roles, plans, and goals), (4) meaning (work is personally important to team members), and (5) impact (team members think their work matters and creates change.

CHAPTER 14

Helpful Hints
Tips from the Meeting Masters

Introduction

Here is some of the best literature on meetings, drawn from the Meeting Masters Research Project and other excellent writings about meetings. This project observed and interviewed individuals who had an outstanding reputation for "giving a meeting" rather than "running a meeting." Their meetings were characterized by authenticity (the issues and choices were real), economy of effort (start on time/end on time), relative brevity (no long, drawn-out sessions), crisp agendas (designed, essentially, like a restaurant menu, except where prices would be on the menu, there are running clock times, with more time given to more difficult items). These individuals were sensitive to the fact that meetings are a graph of energy over time, and energy peaks in the middle of the time period, so the toughest item was in the middle, and a brainstorming discussion of future items was at the end. As one participant said, "You almost feel like a different person; we accomplish so much in Sheila's meetings."

Our articles examine six functions of meetings (with an eye to the critical points where they go wrong) and three important meeting functions, with tools to help them work better. The Garbage Can Model is considered ("where problems, solutions, and participants move from one choice opportunity to another," depending largely on a "relatively complicated intermeshing of elements.") And an argument is made for us to move from individual to collaborative decision-making.

The Essential Idea:
How to Run a Meeting

by Antony Jay

WEB LINK: https://hbr.org/1976/03/how-to-run-a-meeting

Jay contends that despite the fact that meetings can be a waste of time, companies are going to continue to have them. Humankind is a social animal, and if there are no meetings in the places they work, the people's attachment to the organization would be compromised. "Tribal" or informal gatherings would happen instead in pubs, teams, clubs, etc., when work is over.

In this piece, Jay outlines the six main functions of meetings. Their "purpose in the article is to show the critical points at which most meetings go wrong, and to indicate ways of putting them right."

Meetings are of three categories: (1) the assembly: 100 or more people, (2) the council (40–50 people), and (3) the committee (up to 10 people).

The agenda is the most important piece of paper. This can speed and clarify the meeting. Items on the agenda fall into categories such as "1) informative—factual information that could be better circulated in just a document, 2) constructive—originative—something new, 3) executive responsibilities—how do we proceed? 4) legislative framework—'what to do and how to do it.'"

Jay discusses the chairperson's job, which is divided into two tasks, dealing with the subject and dealing with the people. They need to "control the garrulous, draw out the silent, encourage the clash of ideas while discouraging the clash of personalities and watch out for the suggestion-squashing reflex."

Finally, "close on a note of achievement". Even if the final item is left unresolved, refer to an earlier item that was well resolved as you close the meeting and thank the group."

The Essential Idea:
Efficient and Effective Meeting Management and Group Decision-Building: Accomplishing Twice as Much in Half the Time with Higher Quality Decisions
by John E. Tropman

Tropman states "there are only three functions to be performed at meetings: announce (a very few) things, decide about action items, and think about the future through brainstorming." The meeting is organized by the characteristics of the items not the characters in the room!"

Tropman believes in the "Agenda Bell Rule and follows the Urgent Important Grid, which prioritizes items based on importance and urgency. Meeting masters use a menu agenda template, a document that contains a great deal of information in a fairly standard format. It correlates with the Agenda Bell: each item is listed in ascending and descending order of difficulty."

A huge timesaver is to present previous meeting minutes rather than approve the minutes because participants have received them previously and handed in their corrections. Genius! (Although, how many have actually bothered to read them?)

Lastly, Tropman discusses the "boiled frog," "the stumble and bumble," and "the Doom Loop." Let's avoid these, so that unlike the frog, we will know when the water temperature gradually changes, realizing we could actually boil to death.

The Essential Idea: A Garbage Can Model of Organizational Choice
by Michael D. Cohen, James G. March, and Johan P. Olsen

According to our authors,

> "The garbage can process is one in which problems, solutions, and participants move from one choice opportunity to another in such a way that the nature of the choice, the time it takes, and the problems it solves all depend on a relatively complicated intermeshing of elements."

"Four factors were specified which could be expected to have substantial effects on the operation of the garbage can process: the organization's net energy load, energy distribution, its decision structure, and problem access structure. The garbage can model is a first step toward seeing the systemic interrelatedness of organizational phenomena which are familiar, even common, but which have previously been regarded as isolated and pathological."

"It is clear that the garbage can process does not resolve problems well. But it does enable choices to be made and problems resolved, even when the organization is plagued with goal ambiguity and conflict, with poorly understood problems that wander in and out of the system, with a variable environment, and with decision-makers who may have other things on their minds."

The Essential Idea:
A Voice, A Vote, or A Veto
by Howard Teibel

WEB LINK: https://bit.ly/3AyLXuc

Teibel quotes Linda McMillan, former provost of Susquehanna University, Selinsgrove, PA:

"Faculty and administrators in most universities come together daily to accomplish a variety of tasks. However, we do not often perceive ourselves to be 'collaborators.' Frequently, we encounter each other as adversaries, bound to represent our distinctive groups and monitor the behavior of the 'other side.' Thus, we focus on negotiating compromise rather than on collaborating to create the most effective solutions."

According to Teibel, this exemplifies a frequent perception by administrators of their academic colleagues and vice versa.

Teibel Inc. Educational Consultancy and Loyola leadership developed an initiative called the "New Way of Proceeding," a process for gathering broad input to shape revenue-generation ideas and make tough cost-cutting decisions.

The three key leadership bodies representing higher education are: (1) Academic, (2) Administration, and (3) Trustees (public and private boards).

They have different perspectives of each other, which guide how they act and interact with each other. Understanding these differences helps them work in a more collaborative way versus an adversarial way.

Richard Chait shares three guiding principles in leadership, (1) **Consultation:** the opportunity to express one's views, (2) **Communication:** the opportunity to be updated and informed, and (3) **Explanation:** or a commitment to convey the rationale behind decisions. Chait tells us:

> At the heart of these three methods is the principle of transparency or having clarity around who gets to make the decision and then communicate the rationale.

St. Edward's University, University of Colorado Boulder, and Carnegie Mellon University offer their ideas to further connect the institution's stakeholders.

Teibel notes that "one of the main concerns is financial sustainability," the new mantra for the business office. "Faculty are increasingly concerned that their influence in these conversations is diminished, as institutions look more to the bottom line than to the underlying mission."

In Teibel's spirit of driving collaborative decision-making, they believe that three questions guide the dialogue:

1. What problem(s) are we trying to solve?
2. Why is it important to solve them?
3. If we were successful, what would the resolution or new state look like?

Teibel remarks, "Too often collaborative decision-making skips over these three critical questions and instead leaps directly to 'What do we want to do?'"

To take these principles to action and collaboration, we again need communication, consultation, and explanation (or transparency). If possible, we should use events to build on this, i.e., a new president comes in or a new board chair is appointed. As Kelly Fox, CFO of the University of Colorado Boulder, puts it, "When shared governance is working well, the majority of stakeholders understand how decisions are made and are appreciative of the transparency the leadership provides."

The Essential Idea:
The Medium of Managerial Work
from *High Output Management*
by Andrew S. Grove

Peter Drucker stated "that spending more than 25 percent of his time in meetings is a sign of a manager's malorganization." Meetings do get a bad rap. It has been said they can be painful, useless, or downright soul-crushing.

Management will continue to have meetings; so, how do managers use the time in them as effectively and efficiently as possible?

According to Grove, there are two basic kinds of meetings:

1. **The Process-Oriented Meeting**—where knowledge is shared and information is exchanged.
2. **The Mission-Oriented Meeting**—used to solve a specific problem and frequently produce a decision.

Let's first discuss the three kinds of Process-Oriented Meetings Grove refers to.

1. There is a one-on-one meeting with the supervisor and subordinate. These last one hour at a minimum and take place in or near the subordinate's work area. The subordinate will prepare the meeting agenda or outline. The role of the supervisor in a one-on-one is to facilitate the subordinate's view on how things are going. This can be done by applying Grove's "Principle of Didactic Management, Ask one more question!" Just when you think you have heard all your subordinate is going to say, ask another question.

Grove suggests a few helpful hints for effective one-on-one meetings:

- Both have a copy of the meeting outline and take notes on it.
- Establish a "hold" file where both keep issues for discussion at the next meeting.
- Encourage heart-to-heart discussions, but look out for the "zinger"—an end-of-meeting wallop with only a few minutes to deal with it. (Yikes)

2. "The staff meeting is one in which a supervisor and all of his subordinates participate, and which therefore presents an opportunity for interaction among peers." The staff meetings should be controlled with the supervisor keeping things on track and with an agenda given in advance so subordinates can give thought to the meeting.

3. The Operation Review "is the medium of interaction for people who don't otherwise have much opportunity to deal with one another." The basic purpose is to keep the teaching and learning going on between employees that are several organizational levels apart from people and who don't ordinarily meet with each other.

As Grove so aptly put it,

> "One of the distinguishing marks of a good meeting is that the audience participates by asking questions and making comments. You are being paid to attend the meeting, which is not meant to be a siesta in the midst of an otherwise busy day. Regard attendance at the meeting for what it is: work."

The other kind of meeting is the Mission-Oriented meeting.

> "It is usually held ad hoc and is designed to produce a specific output, frequently a decision. The meeting should only have 6–7 people attend, 8 is the cutoff. Decision-making is not a spectator sport, because onlookers get in the way of what needs to be done."

Grove concludes, "The real sign of malorganization is when people spend more than 25% of their time in ad hoc mission-oriented meetings."

References

Cohen, Michael D., 1972. James G. March, and John P. Olsen, "A Garbage Can Model of Organizational Choice," *Administrative Science Quarterly*, Vol. 17, No. 1 (March).

Grove, Andrew S. 1983. "The Medium of Managerial Work. " In *High Output Management*, New York: Random House. Chapter 4, pp. 71–87.

Jay, Antony. 1976. "How to Run a Meeting." *Harvard Business Review*, March.

Teibel, Howard. 2016. "A Voice, A Vote, or A Veto." *Business Officer*, June.

Tropman, John E. "Efficient and Effective Meeting Management and Group Decision Building: Accomplishing Twice as Much in Half the Time with Higher Quality Decisions" (unpublished manuscript).

CHAPTER 15

Helpful Hints from the Decision Maestros

Introduction

The initial material here is from the Meeting Decision Maestros Research Project and includes, as well, some additional outstanding writing.

It turns out that all Meeting Masters are not also Decision Maestros—able to "crystallize" the process into a decision. We use the term "maestro" because decisions involve all elements of the "decision orchestra," so to speak. A decision is a collective product that blends the interests of numerous stakeholders (sections in an orchestra) and produces an overall group project—the performance of various contributions. The Meeting Maestros listened, synthesized, proposed, and then legitimized the decision. It was not always the Master who did this; sometimes it was a member who was especially skilled at this function after listening to the Maestro engage in a summative reflection that organized the contributions and made them seem like a cohesive whole. They then proposed an action that addressed several stakeholder interests, using "decision rules"—norms that made the decision OK—facets such as the breadth of presence, depth of preference, expert and legal opinion, and the boss's preferences—all popular decision rules.

Our articles include a definition of "high-quality" decisions, with suggestions on how to constructively use the criteria, an analysis of Carl Sagan's "Baloney Detection Kit," and the use of "decision trees" to clearly portray the impact of "future alternatives and events." There is an article on the impact of stress on the decision-making process (with some helpful suggestions), a model of decision-making in a "know-how" business, a list of 15 ways to encourage creative idea sharing, and a guide to "idea pitching."

The Essential Idea:
Managing the Decision Process
by John E. Tropman

Tropman notes that while "decisions are the lifeblood of organizational jobs, tasks, and work," many managers "do not think more about the decision-making process, what is involved, and what practices and procedures would make it go better." Tropman describes a "rational decision-making model" where proceeding through "an orderly set of steps" leads to improved outcomes.

Tropman also says "that there is a deeper structure to decision making than most people appreciate," involving building decisions (the decision mosaic) from decision elements through rounds of discussion. At the end of each round (when everyone has said one thing or all those who want to say something have spoken once), decision crystallization occurs. This is a process through which the discussion is pulled together (summative reflection), followed by a suggested action (action idea), and then legitimized (using the five decision criteria). Legitimacy is required because there are conflicting criteria that make decisions OK. These need to be harmonized as the decision crystallizer expresses the suggested action.

Tropman defines a "high quality" decision using an A–F grading matrix, where an "A" decision is (for example, in portfolio analysis) when "all stocks go up, though not equally," with "B," "C," and "D" grades a mixture of good and bad, and an "F" decision is a "catastrophe, also called the nuclear option."

With a goal of an "A" or "B" decision, needs, alternatives, and evidence should be discussed, with gains/losses and pros/cons considered. Decision criteria ("the deeper structure of decision making") are norms that make decisions OK.

Using the criteria can help the process go better and increase the likelihood of a high-quality decision. Decision criteria are norms that make decisions OK. They include several criteria, including

(1) **extensive** (taking into account what most people want);

(2) **intensive** (counteracts drawbacks by going with what people feel strongly about);

(3) **involvement** (giving power to the people who have to carry out the decision);

(4) **expert** (taking into account what the experts have to say);

(5) **power** (what people in power want);

(6) **people not in the room** (what did people not present need or want);

(7) **here-and-now vs. then-and-there** (the difference between now and later);

(8) **the proposal itself** (is it not too costly?);

(9) **not too many moving parts** (keep it simple);

(10) **optics** (will it look OK to the broader community);

(11) **a pilot program** (trying it out); and

(12) **the "social good" criterion** (do you have the right to do the right thing to do?).

Additionally, Tropman offers ideas about (1) managing the decision culture, (2) decision elements and the dominant element, (3) managing the mosaic, (4) rounds of discussion, (5) decision crystallization, and (6) decision sculpting.

The Essential Idea:
The Baloney Detection Kit: Carl Sagan's Rules for Bullshit Busting and Critical Thinking

by Maria Popova

WEB LINK: https://www.themarginalian.org/2014/01/03/
baloney-detection-kit-carl-sagan/

Maria Popova discusses Carl Sagan's "Baloney Detection Kit," a "set of cognitive tools and techniques that fortify the mind against penetration by falsehoods." Sagan also argues that these "tools of healthy skepticism" also apply to everyday life. Sagan shares nine:

> independent confirmation of the facts,
>
> substantive debate on the evidence from all points of view,
>
> relying on experts but not authorities,
>
> spinning more than one hypothesis,
>
> trying not to get overly attached to your own hypothesis,
>
> quantifying (examine any measures or numerical quantities),
>
> examining the links in the chain of argument,
>
> choosing the simpler of two hypotheses, and
>
> asking if the hypothesis can be falsified (i.e., tested).

Sagan felt it is "just as important to unlearn and avoid "the most common pitfalls of common sense." He lists 20 of "the most common and perilous fallacies of logic and rhetoric":

> *ad hominem* (attacking the arguer and not the argument);
>
> argument from authority (trust me, I'm the boss);
>
> argument from adverse consequences (agree, or there will be unacceptable consequences);
>
> appeal to ignorance (whatever is not proven false must be true);
>
> special pleading (you don't understand, "God moves in mysterious ways");
>
> begging the question (presuming you have the right answer);
>
> observational selection ("counting the hits and forgetting the misses");

statistics of small numbers ("I've thrown three sevens in a row. Tonight I can't lose");

misunderstanding the nature of statistics ("everyone I know is above average");

inconsistency (plan for the worst but hope for an unlikely "best");

non sequitur ("it doesn't follow");

post hoc, ergo propter hoc ("it happened after, so it was caused by");

meaningless questions (asking questions that aren't applicable);

excluded middle, or false dichotomy ("are you part of the problem, or part of the solution?";

short-term vs. long-term ("we can't afford ...");

slippery slope (if something is allowed, then something else will follow);

confusion of correlation and causation (inferring cause from a correlation);

straw man (caricaturing a position to make it easier to attack);

half-truths (where some of the evidence is suppressed); and

weasel words (finding "neutral" names for "odious" activities).

Sagan includes a disclaimer:

"Like all tools, the Baloney Detection Kit can be misused, applied out of context, or even employed as a rote alternative to thinking. But applied judiciously, it can make all the difference in the world—not least in evaluating our own arguments before we present them to others."

The Essential Idea:
Decision Trees for Decision-Making
by John F. Magee

Magee quotes Peter F. Drucker's expression of the relationship between present planning and future events: "Long-range planning does not deal with future decisions. It deals with the futurity of present decisions." Magee's "decision tree" concept

> "allows management to combine analytical techniques such as discounted cash flow and present value methods with a clear portrayal of the impact of future decision alternatives and events. Using the decision tree, management can consider various courses of action with greater ease and clarity. The interactions between present decision alternatives, uncertain events, and future choices and their results become more visible."

Magee uses a fictitious company, Stygian Chemical Industries, Ltd., to explore useful aspects of his "decision tree" in several "exhibits:" a cocktail party, chains of actions and events, and financial data, using maximum expected total cash flow as criterion, cash flow analysis, and for simplicity.

Magee begins with a simple example of the decision-tree approach: Imagine plans for an outdoor party. But if it rains, "the refreshments will be ruined, and your guests will get damp." A payoff table—and the decision tree for more complicated situations—are useful to show the routes by which the various possible outcomes are achieved.

Magee notes that a decision tree "of any size will always combine (a) action choices with (b) different possible *events* or *results* of action which are partially affected by chance or other uncontrollable circumstances."

In an appendix, Magee describes two "representative situations."

The Essential Idea:
The Executive Challenge: Managing
Change and Ambiguity
by Michael B. McCaskey

McCaskey's stress model "says that a stress episode begins with the interaction of a person and a disrupting event in the environment." This is followed by an appraisal process that "determines whether a disruption is seen as largely threatening or challenging," and is then followed by a response stage ("at which people either engage, or do not engage, the problem.")

McCaskey notes that "under conditions of high stress, individuals and groups will tend to fixate on one approach to a problem." Individuals and groups then "revert to more primitive cognitive organization (e.g., erratic scanning, a tendency to either/or thinking, seeking less novelty, and rejecting unpleasant messages)." He says that a "favorable reading of the balance of power between self and problem demands will encourage more active coping responses," that the social setting "will influence the appraisal process," and that organizations under stress "try to increase control." Under high stress, "groups will emphasize loyalty and good feelings over problem solving efforts."

> McCaskey lists 12 examples of "troublesome of characteristics":
>
> the nature of the problem is itself in question;
>
> information is problematical;
>
> there are multiple, conflicting interpretations;
>
> there are different value orientations and political/ emotional clashes;
>
> goals are unclear (or multiple and conflicting);
>
> time, money, or attention are lacking;
>
> contradictions and paradoxes appear;
>
> roles are vague and responsibilities unclear;
>
> success measures are lacking;
>
> there is a poor understanding of course-effect relationships;
>
> the symbols and metaphors used can be confusing; and
>
> the participation in decision-making is fluid.

McCaskey encourages managers to "improve their mastery in complex, changing situations" by "appreciating the necessity and usefulness of ambiguity." Ambiguity is valuable because "it can protect options for the future. Decisions, goals, and symbolic slogans … are open for reinterpretation depending upon future needs."

"Since ambiguity raises stress levels for many people, however, managers must try to keep stress within productive levels," which McCaskey says is in the "middle range. Since it is the *perception* of stress that determines performance, managers can work to influence how people appraise the situation. The aim is to have them see the situation as challenging, rather than threatening, and, therefore, in the middle range of perceived stress."

"Managing change and ambiguity calls for a set of skills, attitudes, and personal virtues," including problem-finding, map-building, Janusian thinking ("comfort with acknowledging and constructively using seemingly contradictory beliefs"), controlling and not controlling ("knowing which things can be influenced when"), humor, and charisma.

Other useful skills include problem bracketing (setting aside a fundamental issue that can't be immediately settled), channel switching, dialectical reasoning, nonverbal communication, summary memos, and public recordings.

In a discussion of how to "leverage" these findings, McCaskey suggests selecting people in the core group (the more creativity is needed, the "more heterogeneous and unorthodox group members should be"), framing the problem correctly (not confined to one expert field), setting timetables and standards, and setting judicious deadlines.

"The development of these skills and virtues is a tall order because it is so intricately related to personality." Several things to do: choose staff that add relevant skills that you lack, which of course requires knowing your own weaknesses and then asking staff for help with them. McCaskey believes that managers can improve their own personal skills "if they are willing to make a serious commitment over a number of years."

The Essential Idea: Decisions, Decisions
from *High Output Management*
by Andrew S. Grove

Grove notes that "participating in the process" by which decisions are made is important and essential to every manager and includes decisions from "the profound to the trivial." While in traditional industries, the person making any given decision occupied a particular place in the organizational chart, in businesses "that mostly deal with information and know-how," there is a "rapid divergence between power based on position and power based on knowledge." He explains by saying that graduates hired for their up-to-date knowledge become increasingly less up-to-date as years go by, and they rise up the corporate ladder. He says that "managers get a little more obsolete every day." This requires that the businesses use a different decision-making process, relying on "the middle manager, who not only is a link in the chain of command" but can also assure that the knowledge-holders and power-holders "mesh smoothly."

In Grove's ideal model of decision-making in a know-how business, the first stage is free discussion ("all points of view and all aspects of an issue are openly welcomed and debated.") The next stage is reaching a clear decision ("particular pains should be taken to frame the terms … with utter clarity.") Finally, everyone involved should give the decision their full support (if not necessarily agreement).

Grove says that although this ideal decision-model model seems "an easy one to follow," the author has found that it actually comes easily only to senior managers ("who have been in the company for a long time") and the newly-hired graduates (who "used the model as students doing college work"). For middle managers, this decision-making model is harder to use because they "have trouble expressing their views forcefully," making unpleasant or difficult decisions" or supporting a decision with which they don't agree.

Any decision should be worked out and reached at the lowest competent level where "it will be made by people who are closest to the situation and know the most about it."

The model is also hard to implement because of the peer-group model, in which people are reluctant to state an opinion that might be different from the larger group. People seem more comfortable talking about "our position" than "my position." Grove notes that "you can overcome the peer-group syndrome if each of the members has self-confidence," and has "a gut-level realization that nobody has ever died from making a wrong business decision."

One of the manager's key tasks is to settle six important questions in advance: what decision needs to be made, when does it have to be made, who will decide, who will need to be consulted prior to making the decision, who will ratify or veto the decision, and who will need to be informed of the decision?

If the final decision turns out to be dramatically different from the expectations of the decision-making group, Grove suggests making the announcement, but "don't just walk away from the issue." Grove suggests giving people time to adjust, then reconvening the group later to discuss the decision. "This will help everybody accept and learn to live with the unexpected."

Grove says that good decision-making appears to be complicated because it is. Group decisions do not come easily. "Because the process is indeed onerous, people sometimes try to run away from it." But not every decision can or should be made individually; sometimes there must be a group decision.

The Essential Idea:
15 Ways to Encourage Creative Idea Sharing from All Team Members
by Forbes Communications Council

WEB LINK: https://bit.ly/3ySkWAR

The Forbes Communications Council shared 15 ways to "encourage everyone on your team to bring their campaign to the table," including:

making it personal (start with what you personally care about);

scheduling regular team brainstorms (which creates a "culture of open engagement");

building the right environment (knock down walls and develop a creative environment);

creating innovation zones (keep offices "inviting and open," and possibly a separate innovation area);

being transparent with overall business goals ("the more teams know about changing goals and new opportunities … the more involved they will feel");

asking the team what they want to learn (and then develop a project that encourages their involvement);

creating a rotating culture (switch things up to stimulate new ideas);

building a shared, centralized idea bank (that can be accessed throughout the company);

giving them feedback (show how their work "has produced real results and why");

encouraging mistakes ("making room for them allows for innovative thinking");

outlining campaign objectives (have clear goals and create a safe environment);

fostering cross-functional conversations (bring together members from various departments to "deliver ideation and execution");

feeding their brains (schedule educational activities to discuss during weekly brainstorming meetings);

offering positive reinforcement (encourage good ideas, don't put down bad ideas); and

democratizing idea creation (no idea is dumb, and all ideas are welcome).

The Essential Idea:
This Is How to Pitch Anything
to Anybody—From a Big Promotion
to a Brilliant Idea

by Amanda Berlin

WEB LINK: https://bit.ly/3yPTDXJ

In their "guide for pitching anything to anyone—and getting a yes," Berlin describes seven things to do:

prepare your message ("be ready to answer the all-important question, 'What's in it for me?'");

choose your venue (not en route to a meeting or "at the tail-end of a lunch");

time it wisely (pick the best time for maximum impact, and, if asking for money, ask when there might be available funds);

be clear (what are you asking for, and how can this person facilitate it);

stand behind your idea (and "avoid wishy-washy language" like "This might …");

make it easier to say yes than no (make the next step clear); and

be genuine ("avoid fake smiles, forced laughter, and hyperbole").

References

Berlin, Amanda. 2020. "This Is How to Pitch Anything to Anybody—From a Big Promotion to a Brilliant Idea." themuse.com

Forbes Communication Council. 2018. "15 Ways to Encourage Creative Idea Sharing from All Team Members." Forbes.com, May 21.

Grove, Andrew S. 1983. *High Output Management*. New York: Random House.

Magee, John F. 1964. "Decision Trees for Decision Making." *Decision Making*, July.

McCaskey, Michael B. 1982. *The Executive Challenge: Managing Change and Ambiguity*. Marshfield MA: Pittman.

Popova, Maria. 2017. "The Baloney Detection Kit: Carl Sagan's Rules for Bullshit-Busting and Critical Thinking." Brainpickings.org. https://www3.nd.edu/~ghaeffel/Baloney.pdf.

Tropman, John E. "Managing the Decision Process" (unpublished manuscript).

PART VIII

Bringing Home the Bacon

Evaluation, Implementation, Launch, Institutionalization, and Refurbishment

"My profession has probably been transformed again just since we started this session."

t may be clear by now, but the flow of this book is aimed at promoting timely and positive social and organizational change through proper leadership and management of the meeting and decision process. These are the first two phases. Implementation and institutionalization are the final two, and then the process begins again. The conceptual development of this material began as the Meeting Masters Research Project, with the support of the Meeting Management Institute of the 3M Company. After observing a large number of Masters, it became clear that running a meeting did not always conclude with a high-quality decision, nor, necessarily, any decision (kick the can down the road). But a subset of Meeting Masters was, actually, Decision Maestros. They were able to "close" and orchestrate the accomplishment of Decision-Building.

But the process of constructing high-quality decisions turns out to be only the first two stages of a successful organizational change: stage process. After the decision, came implementation, and, most frequently, a new set of organizational actors become involved: People Who Get Things Done. A new team, with a new set of meetings, begins the process of organizational change. Many organizations fail here because this entire process involves the operationalization of the decision, which then means adjustments to ongoing procedures and practices. The operationalization needs to be checked and then acted upon.

A simple version of this process was developed by W. Edwards Deming and is known as the Plan/Do/Check/Act Model: planning leads to doing, which leads to checking, which leads to acting.

We have some different words, as in the following box:

The Tropman Model	
The Excellent Executive Leader	
1. **Plan**—The New Idea Meeting—Explore and Decide —>Meeting Master	2. **Do**—Decide Decision Maestro
4. **Act**—Launch Organizational Operations Specialist	3. **Check**—Trial Run, Pilot Program, Alpha and Beta Test Implementation Organizational QuarterMaster/ QuarterBack

5. **Organizational Chef**	6. **Institutionalize** Organizational Architects/Carpenters
8. **Launch** Refurbished Program/Policy) **Organizational Mechanic**	7. **Refine—Prune**/Work Out/ Evaluate **Organizational Gardener** Evaluation Expert

Boxes 1–4 are essentially the Deming Model.

Boxes 5–8 refer to:

5. **Creating** the new policy (organizational or program [organizational architects/carpenters]),
6. **Attending** the new program to get the kinks out,
7. **Refining and improving** the policy or program (organizational gardener), and finally
8. **Launching and maintaining** the improved policy (organizational mechanic).

All programs and policies require constant attention; very few things "run themselves."

There is one more position/role that is important in achieving high-quality decisions that lead to high-quality policies, products, programs, and services.

The **Executive Leader** role is comprised of both exceptional leadership skills and exceptional management skills. In a high-quality decisions matrix, the "characteristics" dimension shows leadership as innovative and inventive and management as organized. In **"collaborations,"** leadership includes visionary strategic people, and management includes technical tactical people. In **"crucibles,"** leadership encompasses "crises of direction," an expectation to manage, and management encompasses "crises of operation" and an expectation to lead. In **"competencies,"** leadership includes "reorganization/refocus" and "imagine/envision," and management includes the routine and rational execution of outcomes. In **"conditions,"** leadership involves adhocracy and being "on the balcony," and management involves bureaucracy and being "on the dance floor." In **"contest,"** leadership leverages environment and "looks up and away," and management "looks in and down." In **"change,"** leadership is transformational and management is transactional.

The phrase "executive leader" suggests the substantial differences between executiveship and leadership skill sets. The goal of the excellent executive leader is to "channel switch," with a picture-in-picture. Throughout the day, week, and month they will be switching back and forth, now with the leader picture dominant, now with the manager picture dominant, but (here is where the picture in picture-in-picture comes in) always keeping the other side of the helix in view.

The question might come up, "How does one know which one to use?" After practice, it becomes almost second nature to you, but a rule of thumb is "Do the opposite of what is going well."

This talent is rare because most of us are somewhat better at one than the other, and we tend to do what we are good at. We overuse the leadership muscle and ignore the manager muscle or the reverse. Once this talent is developed you can orchestrate all of the boxes in our high-quality decisions matrix.

We call that a "Rutherford" after a character in Lauren Belfer's *A Fierce Radiance: A Novel* (Belfer 2010) about the development of penicillin manufacture (surely a Grand Challenge). The chief character—Clair—introduces her father, Edward Rutherford, a millionaire who has made his fortune solving complex technical problems.

In one passage, they characterize themselves this way:

> He spent some time in West Virginia working for a coal mining company trying to figure out better methods of ventilation. Went to Texas trying to develop new ways of searching for crude (oil). He had a gift for (identifying and solving) technical problems, a kind of special insight.
>
> **When he was young he thought everybody had that gift. When he was older he realized that nobody else, at least no one he knew, could do what he did.**

The question remains, though: what DID Rutherford do? Belfer does not tell you, but it was probably some combination of these excellent executive leadership skills.

The first skill set comes from a book by Leonard R. Sayles and Margaret K. Chandler called *Managing Large Systems*. What they say applies to building decision-making meetings:

1. Give problems their proper weight and context.
2. Take problems at the right time.
3. Take problems in the right order.
4. Establish and change decision criteria.
5. Act as a metronome setting the organizational pace.

Activating these elements can often be seen as not doing anything; however, they are essential if one is going to move the organization from "bench to bedside," or "art to part."

The second set of requisites comes from a book by Michael McCaskey, *The Executive Challenge: Managing Change and Ambiguity.* The requisites have been slightly adapted here. Excellent executive leaders must all:

1. **Engage in Problem Finding**

   a. Judgment and logic in keying in on the right problem
   b. Taking problems in the right sequence
   c. Engaging in map building
   d. Conceptualizing the problem with a way out

2. **Be Comfortable with Conflicting Value**

   a. Janusian thinking: Looking at a problem from (at least) two sides

3. **Controlling and Noncontrolling**

   a. Assertively going with the flow
   b. Managing the flow
   c. Only dead fish only go with the flow

4. **Problem Bracketing**

   a. Setting a problem aside and then returning

5. **Channel Switching**

   a. Shifting focus completely
   b. While retaining picture-in-picture

To these, we would add:

6. **Evaluation and Refurbishment**

   a. Evaluation of alpha and beta testing

      b. Evaluation after launch
      c. Refurbishment

          i. Honing—smoothing out small imperfections in the process
          ii. Sharpening—taking out the kinks

References

Belfer, Lauren. 2010. *A Fierce Radiance: A Novel*, New York: Harper.

Deming, W. Edwards. 2018. *Out of the Crisis*. Cambridge, MA: MIT Press (reissue).

McCaskey, Michael. 1982. *The Executive Challenge: Managing Change and Ambiguity*, New York: Harper Collins.

Sayles, Leonard R., and Margaret K. Chandler. 1971. *Managing Large Systems*. New York: Harper Row.

CHAPTER 16

Implementation

Introduction

Implementation means turning a decision (policy, solution) into a program or practice. Execution or enactment are also words that are used. In recent times, implementation has become a research field of its own. There is a Society for Implementation Research; its website lists a large number of projects, groups, and resources (https://societyforimplementationresearchcollaboration.org/related-projects-and-conferences/). As we begin our discussion of implementation, a little introduction is necessary. Decisions are the springboard for change. Implementation is change. Yet, the forces for stasis are always powerful, often more so than those for change.

Thus, the executive leader is—like it or not—a change leader. Is it helpful, therefore, to think about the change process and how it can be facilitated structurally. It is helpful, therefore, to know a little about theories of change and what to expect. And the first thing to expect is resistance!

There are lots of resistance-overcoming models. We will mention four:

1. Lewin's 3-stage model (Lewin 1947).
2. The ADKAR Model (Awareness, Desire, Knowledge, Ability, Reinforcement) (Hiatt 2005).

3. Chapter 21 ("The Tactics of Execution: Reducing the Costs of Change" in Simon, Thompson, and Smithburg's *Public Administration* 1991).

4. The "fly on the urinal" theory of change architecture in the book *Nudge* (Thaler and Sunstein 2021).

One of the first things that the Executive Leader does is to establish an implementation team that is usually composed of the various parts and elements of the organization that will be needed to bring the decision into reality. These, of course, involve meetings and decisions. The implementation team usually has different members than the decision team. Sometimes, the implementation team is called a task force to give it a little more organizational oomph. The team often designs a logic model of steps in the new process—how they should work.

A logical model template will have inputs leading to activities leading to outputs leading to outcomes, which are subdivided into short-term, medium-term, and long-term. There should be a process evaluation of activities and outputs, as well as outcome evaluations for each outcome term.

For example, a logic model for program action in program development begins with a situation (its needs and assets, symptoms versus problems, any stakeholder involvement) and a consideration of priorities (mission, vision, values, mandates, resources, local dynamics, collaborators, competitors, and intended outcomes). Inputs are considered (the investment of staff, volunteers, time, money, research base, materials, equipment, technology, partners), then outputs. Output activities include "what we do" (i.e., conduct workshops and meetings, deliver services, develop products, curriculum, or resources, train, provide counseling, assess, facilitate, partner, work with media) and "who we reach" (i.e., participants, clients, agencies, decision-makers, customers) and how satisfied they are. Outcomes (impact) are then considered. Short-term results involve learning (about awareness, knowledge, attitudes, skills, opinions, aspirations, motivations); medium-term results involve action (behavior, practice, decision-making, policies, social action); and long-term or ultimate impacts involve conditions (social, economic, civic, and environmental). Assumptions and external factors should be considered throughout the process, including during a final evaluation phase (which includes focus, collecting data, analyzing and interpreting, and reporting).

An example of this as a flow chart involves car care customer service: The customer enters and checks in. If the needed service does not require an appointment or the customer has an appointment, customer supplies the details and give over the car keys. (Otherwise, an appointment is scheduled). If the customer will wait while the service is performed, they are shown the wait area, then paged or called back to the service area. (If the customer did not wait, they are called and informed). Once the customer returns to the service area, the services performed are reviewed, the customer pays, keys are returned, and the customer leaves.

The next step is a pilot program—a small trial that can be put into place with the idea to explore glitches and impediments.

Once a pilot program is established, it is usually subjected to or should be approached with alpha and beta testing. To use a restaurant example, alpha testing is "back of the house" testing among current staff and trusted advisors. If successful, beta testing follows, which means trying the innovation or invention out with consumers/customers. If that is successful, one proceeds to phase three, launch, at which time the new idea is offered. Institutionalization occurs as the new process or procedure becomes a regular offering.

The Essential Idea: Field Theory in Social Science
by Kurt Lewin

Lewin proposes a three-stage theory of change: Unfreeze-Change-Refreeze. In the UnFreeze phase, they list five tasks:

1. recognize the need for change,
2. determine what needs to change,
3. encourage the replacement of old behaviors and attitudes,
4. ensure there is strong support from management, and
5. manage and understand the doubts and concerns.

Unfreeze is followed by the Change phase, for which Lewin lists three tasks:

1. plan the changes,
2. implement the changes, and
3. help employees to learn the new concept or the new points of view.

This is then followed by the Refreeze phase, which has four tasks:

1. reinforce and stabilize changes,
2. integrate changes into the normal way of doing things,
3. develop ways to sustain the change, and
4. celebrate success.

The Essential Idea:
ADKAR: A Model for Change
in Business, Government,
and Our Community
by Jeffrey M. Hiatt

The ADKAR Model is made up of enablement (sort of like unfreezing) and engagement (sort of like change for Kurt Lewin).

ADKAR stands for Awareness, Desire, Knowledge, Ability, and Reinforcement. Each leads into the next. Awareness, Desire, and Knowledge are in what is called the enablement zone; Ability and Reinforcement, in the engagement zone. In an ADKAR chart, details about each area are given: Under Awareness, "announce the change to employees well ahead of time; explain your reasoning behind the change, including current pain points and potential ROI of the new solution; give employees an opportunity to ask questions and make suggestions." Under Desire, "gauge employees' reactions to the change; identify champions; if employees are resistant or indifferent, address their concerns or show them how the change benefits them personally." Under Knowledge, "provide training or coaching to show what employees need to do after the change takes place; address any skill gaps; offer resources, such as process flowcharts, that employees can reference later on." Under

Ability, "scheduled practice runs before the change is fully implemented; monitor performance immediately following the change and provide constructive feedback; set reasonable goals and metrics at the start; adjust processes as necessary." Under Reinforcement, "monitor the change over time to ensure it fulfills your desired outcome; use positive feedback, rewards, and recognition to encourage employees to keep following the new process."

The Essential Idea:
Tactics of Execution: Securing Compliance

from *Public Administration*

by Herbert A. Simon, Victor A. Thompson, and Donald W. Smithburg

Simon et al. discuss basic steps for planning for the change process along with sensible design suggestions. Simon was an economist (Noble Laureate) and Smithburg and Thompson were political scientists. Their structural suggestions include:

1. considering the inertia costs (make compliance easy and non-compliance difficult, shift the costs of compliance);
2. reducing the moral (cultural) costs (by adjusting the plan to prevailing values and identifying the plan with value symbols);
3. reducing self-interest costs (by minimizing disturbance and provide compensation);
4. reducing rationality costs (by minimizing requirements, developing acceptable justifications, and communicating those justifications); and
5. reducing subordination costs (by employing prestigious spokespersons, etc., and involving those affected in planning).

The Essential Idea: Nudge Theory: 6 Simple Ways to Implement It in a Workplace

by Namrata Borgohain

WEB LINK: https://blog.vantagecircle.com/nudge-theory/

Borgohain describes "nudge theory" as using a "minor feature or suggestion" to influence behavior and decision-making: a "gentle push in the direction of a better option." The theory suggests that a "nudge" is better at modifying behavior than a rule or a threat. The theory's groundwork was laid by Daniel Kahneman and Amos Tversky and popularized in *Improving Decisions About Health, Wealth, and Happiness* by Richard Thaler and Cass Sunstein.

Perhaps the best example of nudge theory is the "urinal fly." A cleaning manager in an Amsterdam airport tried putting fake flies in the men's urinals, giving men something to "aim" at, resulting in an 80 percent reduction in spillage and an eight percent reduction in cleaning costs.

Other examples include ballot bins in London (encourage smokers to "vote" with their cigarette butts, putting the butts into a bin rather than littering with them), Swedish piano stairs (playing music by using the stairs increased stair use by 66 percent), a UK pension experiment (which enrolled employees in a default pension plan rather than waiting for them to pick one), and organ donation (Spain increased the availability of organ donations by making "opt-out" the option, not "opt-in.")

A nudge example from the Covid pandemic: Krispy Kreme offered free doughnuts to people who got vaccinated.

Six simple ways to increase "nudge" in the workplace:

1. keeping healthy snacks at eye level,
2. giving appreciative notes,
3. peer-to-peer recognition,
4. making stairways more visible (to encourage using them instead of the elevator),

5. making rewards and recognition effective, and

6. creating more beautiful workspaces.

The Essential Idea: A Guide to Creating an Implementation Plan in 2022

by Levi Olmstead

WEB LINK: https://whatfix.com/blog/implementation-plan/

Olmstead notes that "bringing a project to life can be tough, and it's even tougher to get it right." But it's even tougher still if you don't have an implementation plan that "outlines the exact path you need to achieve your goal."

Olmstead defines an implementation plan as a "comprehensive outline that explains each and every step you need to take to accomplish an objective or strategic initiative." He suggests eleven steps to creating a good implementation plan:

1. creating a project scope,
2. defining goals,
3. uncovering potential risks,
4. listing assumptions,
5. defining key stakeholders,
6. allocating resources,
7. creating an implementation rollout schedule,
8. going "live" with the change,
9. monitoring the implementation,
10. creating a user adoption strategy, and
11. getting feedback.

Olmstead lists six typical "bumps in the road" to the process:

1. underestimating how long the implementation will take,
2. overlooking details,

3. not allocating enough resources,
4. lacking clear authority or accountability,
5. taking on too much at one time, and
6. having unrealistic deadlines.

The Essential Idea:
6 Steps of Project Implementation
by the Indeed Editorial Team

WEB LINK: https://rb.gy/wrzukp

The Indeed Editorial Team provides six steps toward "project implementation" but first, defines the term as "the process of putting a project plan into action to produce the deliverables" (products or services for clients or stakeholders). The team says it is important because it can "help a team achieve the project objectives while staying within budget and meeting relevant deadlines."

The six steps include:

1. assessing the project plan (making sure it meets the expectations of management, clients, and key stakeholders);
2. executing the plan (including keeping it on schedule);
3. making changes as needed (to keep the project within its scope);
4. analyzing project data (to measure how it is progressing against initial projections);
5. gathering feedback (on what went right and what could be improved next time); and
6. providing final reports.

The Essential Idea:
Difference Between Alpha and Beta Testing
by BYJU's Exam Prep

WEB LINK: https://rb.gy/ahtmz9

"Alpha" testing is called "alpha" because it occurs early in the testing process. "The main focus is simulating real users by making use of white-box and black-box techniques." (In white-box testing, the tester knows the internal structure; in black-box testing, the software is tested without the internal structure being known). "Beta" testing is performed by "real users before a product is shipped to customers, allowing a manufacturer to 'test a product in a real customer's environment.'"

Other differences between alpha and beta testing: the execution cycle of alpha is very long, but short (a few weeks) for beta. "Bugs" can be fixed quickly in alpha, but "bugs" in beta are usually fixed in later versions. While it is mandatory for developers to be present during alpha testing, only end-users are present during beta testing.

The Essential Idea: After-Action Review
by US Agency for International Development

WEB LINK: https://rb.gy/bymtq5

The After-Action Review (AAR) "is a leadership and knowledge sharing tool that helps professionals within USAID and across the partner community to better understand important events, activities, or programs." The report notes that "when administered in a climate of openness, honest discussion, clarity, and commitment to identifying and recommending solutions, the AAR can yield many benefits." They will

> "understand better what was originally intended, what actually happened, what went well and why, and what can be improved and how. Furthermore, the AAR report makes concrete and actionable recommendations for changes and improvements that will impact future success in carrying out this task or similar activities."

The Essential Idea:
Strategy Implementation and Realisation
by Alan Chapman

WEB LINK: https://rb.gy/pxzokw

It is not easy to turn a company's strategies into great business performance. Most companies have great strategic plans but many do not achieve their great plan. "A Fortune Magazine study suggested that 70% of 10 CEO's who fail do so not because of bad strategy, but because of bad execution." Chapman's message is: "effective strategy realisation is key for achieving strategic success."

Chapman defines three essential elements needed to do this:

1. **Motivational Leadership**—REAL leadership is required to compete effectively and deliver growth. People look to leaders to

bring meaning, to make sense of the seemingly unquenchable demand for results, and the need for individuals to find purpose and value.

2. **Turning Strategy into Action**—The ultimate goal is to creatively and systematically bring the strategy to life by creating action plans across an organization that ensures all functions and divisions are aligned behind it.

3. **Performance Management**—To make the strategy "live," **everyone** in the organization needs to take action. Chapman discusses "emotional contracting," which is a crucial and powerful link between the organizational intent, and the motivations, values, and aspirations of the people.

To see if your plan is working, look for business results, progress on targets, KPI (key performance indicators), and look for signs that your people have gotten your corporate message **and** taken it to heart. The story of the group of US Senators visiting NASA when funding was at risk is a great example. One senator asked a man mopping the floor, "So what are you doing here?" The man answered, "I'm here putting a man on the Moon!" All of your company's employees should feel the same vested interest in your company's success. Provided your plan is a good one in the first place, with that type of commitment, how could you possibly fail?

The Essential Idea: The Importance of Business Implementation
by Flora Richards-Gustafson

WEB LINK: https://bit.ly/3aoth5L

Execution is the process of the completion of your grand ideas. They are only ideas unless you can get them implemented so that a concept becomes a reality. Many great ideas are lost or never come to fruition because of all kinds of obstacles. Richards-Gustafson maintains, "Managers should communicate clear goals and expectations, and supply employees with the resources needed to help the company achieve its goals." Good business strategy implementation should set clear priorities on:

- Due dates
- Client needs
- Financial concerns
- Worker needs or logistics—clear action steps and resources

When "what we've got here is failure to communicate" (*Cool Hand Luke* 1967), inefficiency develops and workers can become frustrated, which can lower morale. When deadlines are realistic, people are happier and feel they can succeed at their job. Everyone is happy.

A great implementation plan can move the company forward. Executing your plan well requires good implementation planning. When a company fails to implement or execute well that great idea can be lost, and the company fails to move forward and grow.

References

Borgohain, Namrata. 2021. "Nudge Theory: 6 Simple Ways to Implement It in A Workplace." *Vantage Circle* (blog), December. https://blog.vantagecircle.com/nudge-theory/.

BYJU's Exam Prep. No date. "Difference Between Alpha and Beta Testing." byjus.com.

Chapman, Alan. 2017. "Strategy Implementation and Realisation. Businessballs.com, June.

Flora Richards-Gustafson, Flora. 2019. "The Importance of Business Implementation." Chron.com, April.

Hiatt, Jeffrey M. 2006. *ADKAR: A Model for Change in Business, Government, and Our Community.* Fort Collins, CO: ProSci Research, 2006.

Indeed Editorial Team. 2021. "6 Steps of Project Implementation." Indeed.com, May 20. https://www.indeed.com/career-advice/career-development/project-implementation.

Lewin, Kurt. 1947. *Field Theory in Social Science.* New York: Harper & Row.

Levi Olmstead. 2021. "A Guide to Creating an Implementation Plan in 2022." Whatfix.com, September 27. https://whatfix.com/blog/implementation-plan/.

Simon, Herbert A., Victor A. Thompson, and Donald W. Smithburg. 1991. *Public Administration.* Abingdon, Oxon: Routledge.

Thaler, Richard H., and Cass R. Sunstein. 2021. *Nudge: The Final Edition.* London: Penguin Books.

US Agency for International Development. 2006. "After-Action Review." https://pdf.usaid.gov/pdf_docs/PNADF360.pdf?msclkid=d4ed2670b44711eca3661a433804f3d2.

CHAPTER 17

The Evaluation

Introduction

Because "evaluation" occurs after a period of time, it is almost always at the "end" of some intervention or programmatic episode or time frame. After Implementation has been completed, and the program and service are running, organizations forget about it until something "hits the fan." Then, there is a flurry of excitement, and lots of work "fixes" (often quick fixes) are introduced and the whole organization collapses until the next crisis arises, which due to sloppy work on the just-mentioned repair, is all too soon, which, in turn, leads to a round of finger-pointing. Someone is fired. Unfortunately they were just the messenger of the problem and things get worse. The door to the Doom Loop has just opened.

Sometimes, organizations call on universities to assist in the evaluation. The problem here is (at least) seven fold:

1. "evaluation" goals should be put in at the beginning (it often is not);
2. involving professors in knowledge development (they are often interested in different questions than the agency is, leading to contractual and financial conflicts);
3. there is often a dispute between outcome measures (we did this and that) and outcome measures (we accomplished this and that ... or not) because describing "activities" is easier than showing "results";
4. evaluation assessment and research proceed along very different timelines and have very different assessment cultures of their own;

5. many organizations do not have evaluation staff of their own who can liaise with the academic temporary workers (hence, the cultural gap);

6. organizations often need special resources (for corporate organizations: the finance department, for nonprofits: foundations), which adds a "third player" to further complicate evaluation; and

7. what is "being evaluated" is an operating program, not a double blind assessment, so issues come up and changes are made along the way, often frustrating the professors.

So, it is a rocky road ahead.

Several techniques for evaluation can provide useful perspectives.

Starting with the end in mind (Covey 2020) and organizing backward is extremely effective. The evaluation plan is integral to the implementation plan.

In cooking big pieces of meat (including turkey and standing rib), you take the temperature along the way. There are poke-in thermometers that provide constant information. Do this with your new program, and start "taking its temperature" from the beginning.

Talk with others who have similar programs. There is no point in reinventing the wheel. Be sure to converse with other organizations with similar or analogous problems. It is amazing what you learn.

Decisions do not implement themselves. There is a need for an implementation team. It is especially important that there is a carryover from the decision group because if the implementation team is made up of all new players, much can be "lost in translation."

The Essential Idea: Improve Your Teamwork with "Keep/Stop/Start"

by Ariel Group

WEB LINK: https://rb.gy/de26pd

The Ariel Group describes "Keep/Stop/Start" as a "quick, easy, low-risk debriefing technique" that is useful in many business applications, including teamwork, idea generation, problem-solving, and sales effectiveness. The process begins with team members defining "the issues affecting the quality of their collaboration" and then developing "practical ways to work better together." The "Keep" list contains "those things that the team should continue to do to be effective." The "Stop" list contains "counterproductive practices and process gaps that reduce team effectiveness." The "Start" list contains "new, creative solutions to often vexing, long-term problems."

What makes the Keep/Stop/Start model such a powerful tool is that everyone on the team contributes "to the change mandate." The Ariel Group encourages focus on behaviors (team process and procedures), not on assumed attitudes and motivations; for ending the meeting with "tangible, accountable next steps"; and for planning for group follow-up meetings (to ensure implementation and to anticipate any "mid-course" corrections).

The Essential Idea: KISS (Keep It Simple, Stupid)— A Design Principle
by Interaction Design Foundation

WEB LINK: https://bit.ly/3xCtdIx

Keep It Simple Stupid (KISS) has a long history. An early version of this idea is called Occam's Razor: The Bishop of Occam (fourteenth century) formulated a rule to differentiate among competing mathematical proofs.

His rule, which survives to this day, was that the solution with the fewest steps wins.

KISS focuses on the idea that "if we can't understand a product, we can't use it properly." Common variants include "Keep It Short and Simple" and "Keep It Simple and Straightforward." The article notes several famous "alternatives" to KISS, including Occam's Razor, but also Einstein's quote, "Make everything as simple as possible but not simpler," and Da Vinci's quote, "Simplicity is the ultimate sophistication."

The authors caution "not to make things too simple" so that it doesn't interfere with the objective.

The Essential Idea:
The Sufficient-Component
Cause Model
by Wayne W. LaMorte

WEB LINK: https://bit.ly/3aKBot7

LaMorte describes the "sufficient-component cause model," which was developed to help provide a general model for "the conditions necessary to cause (and prevent) disease." This model has similarities to the two-cause model described by Tropman in his chapter introduction: "outcomes have multiple contribution determinants that may act together to produce an event." The model proposes that a single factor is insufficient "sufficient cause" for an event to occur and that a "minimum set of factors and circumstances," if present, will produce the event.

Using a medical example, LaMorte notes that a sufficient cause for AIDS might include (1) exposure to an infected individual, (2) engaging in "risky" sexual behavior with that individual, and (3) the absence of antiretroviral drugs. LaMorte says that "if any of these components were absent, AIDS could not occur."

In a decision-making and decision-implementation setting, this model might suggest that there is a "minimum set of factors and circumstances" that must be present for a good decision and its successful implementation to occur. It also suggests that these factors are knowable and usable rather than arrived at blindly or without planning.

The Essential Idea:
The Ishikawa Chart (Fishbone Diagram)
by Kaoru Ishikawa

One way to approach precipitating/predisposing causality is to use an Ishikawa chart/fishbone diagram, which was popularized in the 1960s. Ishikawa developed the chart from a concept first used in the 1920s, and it is considered one of the seven basic tools of quality control. Ishikawa pioneered "quality management processes" in the Kawasaki shipyards in Japan.

It is also known as a fishbone diagram because of its shape: the center of the diagram has a fish skeleton, head pointed to the right. The "head" is labeled as the "defect" to be considered. The perceived "causes" of the defect are listed in series of "ribs" above and below the skeleton. The "causes" above the skeleton are "major causes," and the ones below are the "root causes."

Advantages to the diagram include: (1) the highly visual nature of the diagram can spark further brainstorming about root causes, (2) it allows all causes to be viewed simultaneously, and (3) it quickly shows if a root cause is found multiple times.

The diagram below (assembled by Dan Madaj) illustrates the multiplicity of causes by typical categories so that one can be sure that all the relevant information is included in the diagnosis.

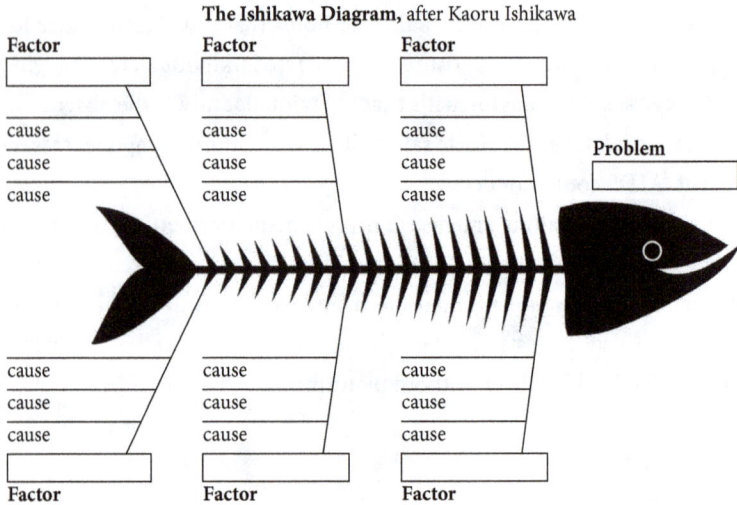

The Ishikawa Diagram, after Kaoru Ishikawa

Factor	Factor	Factor
cause	cause	cause
cause	cause	cause
cause	cause	cause

Problem

cause	cause	cause
cause	cause	cause
cause	cause	cause

Factor	Factor	Factor

FIGURE 17.1

The Essential Idea:
The Meeting Is Over. Now It's Time to Evaluate and Improve!

by IToolkit.com

WEB LINK: https://bit.ly/3zpmAKV

"Every meeting is a process, and evaluation makes the process complete." All meetings need a "postmeeting review." This will decide whether the meeting was a success and met the purpose of your meeting.

To evaluate your meeting and see if it has met your expectations, four key performance factors should be reviewed.

1. Meeting Results
2. Meeting Process

3. Participation/Tone
4. Next steps

Questions need to be answered in the four areas. Examples would include:

- **Meeting Results**—Did you meet the objectives you set out to accomplish? Did you make decisions that made the meeting necessary in the first place?
- **Meeting Process**—Did the meeting logistics work? Did you keep the meeting within your allotted time frame? Did the meeting drag on too long, with everyone disengaged by the meeting's end? Was the correct venue, phone conference, or zoom meeting vs. physical meeting used? Was your meeting well attended?
- **Participation/Tone**—Did everyone participate in a positive and productive manner? Did one person try to hijack the meeting in a self-serving or negative way? If so, how can you avoid that in the future?
- **Next Steps**—Moving forward, what items need to be addressed, documented, and followed up on? Does everyone understand their specific role(s) in reaching the goals and expectations decided in the meeting? How will this be monitored for success?

When all this is completed, put the results to use in the file of lessons learned. Now, it is time for your next meeting.

The Essential Idea:
Stop Wasting People's Time with Meetings
by David Lancefield

WEB LINK: https://rb.gy/5ewphh

Everyone should have a strategy for their meetings. Lancefield discusses 5 Strategies to showcase your best self to your colleagues and have productive meetings.

1. "Articulate Your Ambition Clearly"

   a. Remind people what they are there to do. Encourage folks to call out clarifications or disagreements before the meeting. Explain the urgency of the discussion in relation to the company strategies. Put attendees in a positive state of mind by reminding them of your belief in their abilities. Work out how YOU want to show up.

2. "Decide What Roles You Want to Play"

   a. Lancefield discusses the roles of the Catalyst, Custodian, Challenger, Convener, and Decision-maker. Who do you want to be today?

3. "Work Out Your Most Distinctive Contribution"

   a. Know what you are good at. What are your strengths? Create "profiles" of other meeting participants that you might for your customers. This helps you learn your team.

4. "Use Signals Wisely"

   a. Use both your own signals and picking up on other people's interests and intentions.

5. "Manage Yourself in the Moment"

   a. Keep your composure no matter the circumstance to think clearly and communicate effectively

   b. You can make more strategic choices about how to manage yourself in the moment by being clear about your focus; picking your battles; anticipating the triggers and the "triggerers." "I'll come to you after I've finished my point"; labeling your reaction "meta-awareness" (breathing techniques, center yourself, etc.); refocusing your attention; reminding yourself of your ambition; and focusing and reframing the discussion by refocusing attention on different ways to address the issues at hand.

According to Lancefield, "practicing these 5 Strategies will help you be more intentional with your actions and more likely to bring your best self to the discussion." Now stop wasting my time!

The Essential Idea: Why Your Meetings Stink—and What to Do About It
by Steven G. Rogelberg

WEB LINK: https://hbr.org/2019/01/
why-your-meetings-stink-and-what-to-do-about-it

Many meetings are referred to as a "time suck." Feedback indicates that managers fail in one critical area, leading effective meetings. Of the 23 hours that executives spend in meetings each week, eight hours are unproductive. That is almost 25% of your time spent. So, what can we do about it?

Let's start with the leader. Most often, leaders think they are doing a fantastic job. The leaders are usually the ones who talk the most, so they assume things are going well. Not necessarily so. While attendees are complaining and frustrated—a phenomenon called "meeting recovery syndrome," the leaders are patting themselves on the back. Leaders need to have more "self-awareness," objectively assess and improve their own meeting skills, and make positive changes.

Rogelberg believes this is how:

1. **Assessment**—Self-observation—Take a few minutes after each meeting to reflect on how it went. Get feedback from others. Identify your key strengths and weaknesses and create a plan for improvement.
2. **Preparation**—Know exactly why you are meeting, and define your goals to set the stage for achieving them. Decide who really

needs to be there. Focus on time and place. For example, move to a different venue, meet in the morning instead of the afternoon, meet for 50 minutes instead of an hour. Suggest a walking meeting or a short, standing meeting.

3. **Facilitation**—Start as soon as attendees enter the room. Leaders acknowledge people at the door, express gratitude for their time, play music, offer snacks, and ask folks to turn OFF their phones and laptops. Start with a good opening statement explaining why the meeting was called. "Brainwriting" is also discussed. (Have individuals quietly reflect and write down their ideas before sharing them out loud; research shows that this approach yields more creative thinking than brainstorming does).

4. **Reassessment**—Even when the first three things are observed, there will always be room for improvement, so keep repeating the process.

The Essential Idea:
What Is an Organisational Performance Evaluation?

by Wevalgo.com

WEB LINK: https://bit.ly/3zsin96

An article by Wevalgo.com discusses nine types of organizational performance evaluation "diagnoses," "categorized according to two key criteria": approach used, and skills required:

1. machine—workstation (an analysis of the performance of a machine or workstation);
2. process (analysis of work processes involving several "actors");
3. leadership (based on interviews with managers, specific tests, and, possibly, surveys);
4. information systems (diagnostics usually carried out during installation or "a major evolution");

5. organizational diagnostics (identify areas for improvement as well as causes of performance losses);
6. scoping (an initial or preliminary evaluation to help define and specify a direction to take);
7. organizational audit (an assessment of practices against a pre-defined standard);
8. restructuring; and
9. cost killing (when the main objective is cost reduction, "opportunities" must be imperative enough to withstand a loss of competitiveness or another significant deficit).

References

Ariel Group. 2020. "Improving Your Teamwork with 'Keep/Stop/Start.'" Arielgroup.com, October. https://binged.it/3zHAzM2.

Covey, Stephen R. 2020. *The 7 Habits of Highly Effective People: 30th Anniversary Edition*. Simon and Schuster.

Interaction Design Studio. 2021. *KISS (Keep It Simple, Stupid)—A Design Principle*. Interaction Design Foundation.

Ishikawa, Kaoru. 1976. *Guide to Quality Control*. Asian Productivity Organization.

ITtoolkit.com. n.d. "The Meeting Is Over. Now It's Time to Evaluate and Improve!" *i.t.Toolkit Magazine*.

LaMorte, Wayne W. 2019. "The Sufficient-Component Cause Model." *Boston University: School of Public Health*, January. https://bit.ly/3aKBot7.

Lancefield, David Lancefield. 2022. "Stop Wasting People's Time with Meetings." *Harvard Business Review*, March 14.

Rogelberg, Steven G. 2019. "Why Your Meetings Stink—and What to Do About It." *Harvard Business Review*, January–February. https://hbr.org/2019/01/why-your-meetings-stink-and-what-to-do-about-it.

Wevalgo.com. 2021. "What Is an Organisational Performance Evaluation?" Wevalgo.com.

SUMMATIVE REFLECTION

I f you've skimmed or read your way through this book, hopefully, you've been amused but also inspired, particularly by the realization that meetings can be made more efficient (doing them right) and effective (accomplishing appropriate and high-quality decisions in them)!

Over the course of 67 articles and book synopses, we've gathered a collection of humorous articles on meetings, then expanded the focus to look at what goes wrong in meetings but also what goes right, with some suggestions for further improvement.

Maybe in the future when you or a colleague complains about a dull or unproductive meeting, rather than "piling on" you'll take a moment to think about what could be changed … and how. You can step in, not on or over.

Keep in mind that organizational change is like maintaining your garden: it requires constant gardening, or the weeds of bad practices will creep back in.

SUMMATIVE REFLECTION

INDEX